# Confederate General
# STEPHEN ELLIOTT

*Beaufort Legend, Charleston Hero*

D. MICHAEL THOMAS

FOREWORD BY NEIL BAXLEY, HISTORIAN

Published by The History Press
Charleston, SC
www.historypress.com

Copyright © 2020 by D. Michael Thomas
All rights reserved

*Cover images*: Library of Congress.

First published 2020

Manufactured in the United States

ISBN 9781467144797

Library of Congress Control Number: 2019951874

*Notice*: The information in this book is true and complete to the best of our knowledge. It is offered without guarantee on the part of the author or The History Press. The author and The History Press disclaim all liability in connection with the use of this book.

All rights reserved. No part of this book may be reproduced or transmitted in any form whatsoever without prior written permission from the publisher except in the case of brief quotations embodied in critical articles and reviews.

*This book is for my wife, DeeDee, and is dedicated to the memory of her second great-grandfather Albert D. Goodwin, and his brother William, privates in Company D, Twelfth Battalion, Georgia Light Artillery. Both served valiantly at Fort Sumter under command of Major Stephen Elliott Jr. during its Second Great Bombardment in late 1863. It was there that Albert was wounded by an enemy shell fragment, his only wound in nearly four years of arduous service.*

*The bravest are surely those who have the clearest vision of what is before them, glory and danger alike, and notwithstanding, go out to meet it.*
—*Thucydides*

*You have power over your mind—not outside events.
Realize this and you will have strength.*
—*Marcus Aurelius*

# CONTENTS

Foreword, by Neil Baxley ............................................. 9
Preface ....................................................................... 11
Acknowledgements .................................................... 13

1. The Halcyon Days (1830–1860) ........................... 15
2. War! (1861) ............................................................ 17
3. Year of Transition (1862) ..................................... 26
4. Changes Abound (January–August 1863) ........... 38
5. Post of Honor: Fort Sumter (September–December 1863) ... 53
6. Post of Honor: Fort Sumter (January–April 1864) ... 85
7. On to Virginia (May–June 1864) .......................... 90
8. Petersburg and The Crater (July–August 1864) ... 98
9. The Final Campaign (September 1864–April 1865) ... 102
10. The Guns Go Silent (May 1865–February 1866) ... 110

Epilogue ..................................................................... 115
Appendix A ................................................................ 121
Appendix B ................................................................ 123
Notes .......................................................................... 127
Bibliography .............................................................. 137
Index .......................................................................... 141
About the Author ...................................................... 143

# FOREWORD

Beaufort, South Carolina, is a small coastal town in the southeastern corner of the state. It is a town steeped in history. The French, the Spanish and the English vied for control of this small outpost. Throughout its history, its sons have gone forth in the service of their state and their country.

Located in the heart of downtown Beaufort is St. Helena's Anglican Church, a brick edifice built in 1715. The churchyard is surrounded by a brick wall built as a defensive measure that encompasses a full city block. Inside that city block lie the graves from many of the most influential families in Beaufort history. Each side of the wall has a gate located midway down the block. When you enter the gate on the north wall, your view will settle on a tall obelisk, the largest monument in the churchyard. Closer investigation reveals that it and nearly a dozen markers around it bear the same last name, *Elliott*. The obelisk bears the name *Stephen*.

Stephen Elliott was born in Beaufort to a wealthy family. He enjoyed privilege, growing up with the best that Beaufort and his family had to offer: a nice home and a quality education. After being admitted to the bar in South Carolina, he was elected to the state House of Representatives. He understood that he was expected to serve the citizens of South Carolina. In December 1860, the governor of South Carolina called in his marker.

Stephen Elliott was ready and willing to answer the call. He volunteered to join the fledgling Confederate army. Over the next four years, Stephen Elliott would pay the marker in full. He would be wounded multiple times.

# Foreword

As the war progressed, Elliott's abilities were recognized by each of his commanders. Beginning the war as a captain, he was eventually promoted to brigadier general.

Not only was Stephen wounded several times, but he was also in the center of several of the more influential events of the war in the East. Elliott never shirked from his duty, even after being severely wounded. He remained at his post, giving orders and organizing the defense and counterattack at the Crater until the situation was stabilized. It was this wound that would finally lead to Stephen Elliott's death in 1866. But before he succumbed to the wound, he was reelected to the seat in the South Carolina House of Representatives that he had held on the day war was declared.

The City of Beaufort remembers Stephen Elliott in a variety of ways. The local chapter of the United Daughters of the Confederacy bears his name. A very popular park located on the bluff of the Beaufort River, in downtown Beaufort, also bears his name. There is one street named Elliott. On the Marine Corps Recruit Depot Parris Island, the training area where Marine recruits undergo gas-chamber training is named Elliott's Beach and is known throughout the Marine Corps as "E" beach. This is because, prior to 1861, the Elliott family owned the entire island.

The Elliott family and General Stephen Elliott left a mark on Beaufort County that has been fondly remembered through the years. It is well-nigh time that Brigadier General Stephen Elliott received a biography to memorialize his story for posterity. This edition will fit that bill nicely.

Neil Baxley
Beaufort, South Carolina
Author of *No Prouder Fate: The Story of the 11$^{th}$ South Carolina Volunteer Infantry* and *Walk in the Light: The Journey of the 10$^{th}$ and 19$^{th}$ South Carolina Volunteer Infantry*

# PREFACE

My interest in General Stephen Elliott Jr. began in 2018 while reading an article about the 1864 Battle of the Crater at Petersburg. It dawned on me that I knew nothing about him other than what happened in this bloody engagement. Out of sheer curiosity, I began seeking material on Elliott. I quickly learned that there was no biography or other in-depth study pertaining to him, and my disappointment led me to other sources. One of those was *The War of the Rebellion: A Compilation of the Official Records of Union and Confederate Armies*, where an enormous amount of material on Elliott is found. As I was prompted to go further, searches were conducted on each of his three separate service records, where, again, an impressive amount of information relating to his military career was readily available. Taken together, these two sources provided a superb basis for review of his involvement in the War Between the States. While studying these primary sources, a mental image of the man began forming in my mind, one shaped not only by his obvious courage, boldness and leadership ability, but also by the respect and admiration so freely given by his superior officers. Other bona fide sources, including a cache of his wartime letters to his beloved wife, Charlotte, were located during a lengthy search and proved most valuable by adding details not found elsewhere. In time, the realization hit me that sufficient data was in hand to write a book on this distinguished soldier and that he was indeed more than worthy of having his story told.

# Preface

This, then, is the first full-length study of General Stephen Elliott Jr., a Lowcountry legend and hero to the citizens of South Carolina. His personal valor, boldness and superb leadership as a captain of artillery who also led partisan raids against his blue-coated foe left lasting impressions on those under whom he served. Such notables as Generals William S. Walker, P.G.T. Beauregard and Robert E. Lee quickly recognized his soldierly abilities, and each later displayed immense respect for him. Confederate president Jefferson Davis was impressed sufficiently with Elliott's service at Fort Sumter in late 1863 to issue an executive order promoting him to lieutenant colonel.

Handpicked by Beauregard in 1863 to command, and hold, Fort Sumter in Charleston's harbor during the darkest of times, Elliott proved himself worthy of this trust. In doing so, he became a revered symbol of Southern resolve. His name was conspicuously mentioned in newspapers across the entire South and beyond. Rising to colonel of infantry and, shortly after, to general commanding a full brigade, Elliott continued to perform well. Wounded in action on at least five separate occasions in the war, he faithfully answered the call of duty from his state and his nation until the guns went silent in 1865. Returning to Beaufort with his health shattered and his property seized, he began the difficult and challenging task of recovering from his misfortunes. With tireless energy and his good name, he was on the path of recovery when, less than a year afterward, he passed away at age thirty-five. His untarnished legacy lives on.

In presenting Elliott's military service, I deemed it critical to place certain experiences in their proper context by including amplifying details germane to some of these key events. A full understanding and appreciation of his service cannot be obtained without knowing some of the background circumstances influencing his actions, decisions or involvement at certain critical junctures. They provide the context needed to illuminate Elliott's service and answer the "who, why and how" questions a reader might have. Efforts have been made to present these and other scenarios in the simplest, most concise form possible for this work to retain clarity and remain focused on Stephen Elliott Jr. Many fine books have been written on some of the major actions in which Elliott was involved and can easily be found by those wishing to learn more about them.

# ACKNOWLEDGEMENTS

It is a great pleasure to acknowledge those providing substantial assistance during the search for material on Stephen Elliott Jr. and afterward. Without their contributions, the work would have been much more difficult. Each was exceedingly gracious and encouraging.

I am sincerely grateful to Mrs. Anita Henson, president of the Stephen Elliott Chapter No. 1349, United Daughters of the Confederacy, for her support and guidance when seeking local sources of assistance in Beaufort. She set me on the right track.

Special thanks go to Grace Cordial, MLS, SL, CA, manager of the Beaufort District Collection, the special local history and archives of Beaufort County Library. Her updated listing of related links and materials relating to Stephen Elliott Jr. was most helpful.

The special consideration and assistance provided by Mary Lou Brewton and the Beaufort History Museum Board of Directors was of immense value and is cheerfully acknowledged.

Appreciation also goes to Robert E.L. Krick, historian at Richmond National Battlefield Park, for patiently guiding me through the administrative processes and promotion policies of the Confederate army.

My good friend Michele Armstrong contributed in a big way. Her keen observations and helpful critiques were of immense value.

I am deeply indebted to Neil Baxley, a lifelong historian who provided the foreword to this work. His support from the start of this work has been informative and encouraging, and for that, I will always be grateful. Neil, a

## Acknowledgements

Marine Corps veteran who has lived in Beaufort for decades, is recognized as a preeminent historian and authority on the history of the Beaufort area from its earliest days as well as its long list of notable citizens. In addition to writing two fine regimental history books pertaining to South Carolina's "Men in Gray," he has given numerous lectures on Beaufort's local history and presented living history demonstrations for area schools, historical societies and other organizations. His work on the 250-year history of the Beaufort County Sheriff's Department is nationally recognized and has led to lectures on it across the nation.

Hearty thanks to my editor, Rick Delaney, whose keen eye, gentle guidance and patience are greatly appreciated.

Finally, I gratefully acknowledge the full support and encouragement freely given by my wife, DeeDee. She traveled with me every step of the way, offering thoughtful, helpful insights and suggestions.

*1*
# THE HALCYON DAYS (1830-1860)

Stephen Elliott Jr. was born in Beaufort in October 1830, the first child of Reverend Stephen and Ann Hutson Habersham Elliott. Over the next thirteen years, the family grew with the addition of four more sons and a daughter. After Ann's death in 1843, Reverend Elliott remarried and fathered two more children.

Stephen's forefathers had made their mark in the South Carolina Lowcountry, the coastal area between Charleston and Savannah. Since the arrival of Thomas Elliott in the early 1690s, the following generations of Elliotts each secured large landholdings and were politically astute. Stephen's father was an 1824 graduate of Harvard University and a successful, wealthy plantation owner. His grandfather William Elliott III is credited with bringing long staple cotton to Beaufort. More commonly known as sea island cotton, it became a most prized and coveted crop renowned for its high-quality fiber.

In the early 1830s, Stephen's father felt called to the ministry. After completing his studies, the Reverend Stephen Elliott Sr. became an ordained Episcopal priest in 1836. Though retaining his plantation, he dedicated the rest of his life to preaching the Gospel throughout the Lowcountry. He devoted substantial missionary work toward the Negro population, as did many other clergymen, using his personal wealth to support his work.[1]

Stephen flourished in the natural environment afforded by the rivers, tidal creeks and streams around the various islands surrounding Beaufort and Port Royal Sound, the gateway to the Atlantic Ocean. He gained a reputation as a skilled fisherman and sailor familiar with tides, currents and shoals of the area. His education was sufficient to enter Harvard as a young man, but he transferred to South Carolina College in Columbia, from which he graduated in 1850. Four years later, he married Charlotte Stuart and took on the responsibilities of establishing and supporting a family.

The next six years were productive ones for Stephen. By 1860, he and Charlotte were the proud parents of three young boys. He was successful as a planter and owned real estate valued at $15,000, much of it on Parris Island, and claimed a personal estate of $25,000.[2] In 1856, his leadership abilities led him to being elected captain of the Beaufort Volunteer Artillery, a militia unit dating from the Revolutionary War, after having previously served as first lieutenant.[3] In November 1859, he was elected a member of South Carolina's Forty-Fourth General Assembly for a two-year term representing St. Helena's Parish in the Beaufort District and appointed to the Military Affairs Committee.[4] All in all, these were years of success with much promise for the future.

However, the 1850s was a decade troubled with rumblings of national discord and discontent on a variety of issues. Talk of secession became more pronounced, leading to fears of war. Though leaders from the South and North argued the issues at length, the results were disheartening. Nothing changed the path toward disunion. Stephen and his militia company commenced drilling with their state-issued cannon in earnest. Stephen learned the fine points relating to an artillery battery under the tutelage of a previous captain, a West Point graduate, and by 1860, the Beaufort Volunteer Artillery members understood they might well soon be involved in warfare.[5]

The issue of secession reached a boiling point with the election of Abraham Lincoln on November 6, 1860, despite his receiving less than 40 percent of the ballots cast. On November 24, Stephen wrote a letter to South Carolina's governor, W.H. Gist. He wrote that, by a unanimous vote, the Beaufort Volunteer Artillery, "having a battery of six pieces, tender our services as volunteers to the Secession."[6] The next month, South Carolina seceded from the Union and braced for the future.

2

# WAR! (1861)

South Carolina was followed quickly in secession by six other states. Together, these states formed the Confederate States of America. Tensions heightened in the early part of the year as focus on Fort Sumter in Charleston's harbor increased. Following Lincoln's inauguration on March 4, 1861, Southern hopes for a peaceful parting were dashed by his decision to send the infamous Fox Expedition with supplies and reinforcements to Sumter the next month. This provocation led Confederate authorities to respond before the expedition arrived. On April 12, bombardment of the fort began after a demand for its surrender was refused by the garrison commander. The next day, however, the fort capitulated and the garrison was transferred to the ships of the Fox Expedition waiting offshore, having arrived too late to carry out its mission. On April 15, Lincoln called for seventy-five thousand men to quell "the rebellion," and the War Between the States was formally begun. Four more states subsequently left the Union to join the Confederacy, and both sides began preparation for the coming hostilities.

Stephen Elliott Jr. and his four brothers had decisions to make. Stephen, age thirty, cast his fortunes with the Beaufort Volunteer Artillery, which was formally mustered into state service on May 3, 1861, as Company A of the Eleventh South Carolina Volunteer Infantry Regiment. John, twenty-eight years old and a lawyer, was exempt from military service because he previously had entered training as an Episcopal clergyman. Ralph, twenty-six and a physician, enrolled in the Palmetto Guard, later designated

Company I, Second Palmetto Regiment, as a private. William, twenty-two, had been a member of the Brooks Guard Volunteers several months before the firing on Fort Sumter in April. His command actually participated in the firing on Sumter and was one of the units to occupy the fort immediately after it surrendered. The command became Company K, also in the Second Palmetto Regiment, and he was elected first lieutenant. Both Ralph and William left Charleston in early May with their respective companies destined for Virginia. Middleton Elliott, Stephen's youngest brother and just nineteen, was a rising senior at the Military College of South Carolina (The Citadel) and was selected to serve as a cadet drillmaster over the summer for a newly formed regiment in Georgetown, South Carolina.[7] Their half brother, Henry D. Elliott, at the tender age of twelve, remained at home. The Beaufort Volunteer Artillery, with other arriving units, initially mustered, drilled and trained in the vicinity of Hardeeville, South Carolina. However, on June 12, the unit was officially mustered into Confederate service at Bay Point at the entrance of Port Royal Sound.[8]

On May 19, Elliott and sixteen others of the Beaufort Volunteer Artillery, while it was still a South Carolina militia unit, were involved in a naval operation and experienced their first act of hostilities. Lieutenant Thomas Pelot, a gallant and aggressive Confederate naval officer, advised Elliott that he intended to take his ship *Lady Davis* to seek and engage the U.S. warship *Perry*, which was known to be lurking in the area. Pelot asked Elliott to be his pilot and to bring a detachment of his artillery unit to act as marines, to which Elliott readily agreed. Delayed by bad weather one day, the *Lady Davis* set out on its mission, but *Perry* was nowhere to be found. Instead, a merchant ship flying the U.S. flag, *A.B. Thompson*, was encountered and seized as a war prize off Savannah. With Elliott acting as his pilot and members of the Beaufort Volunteer Artillery guarding the crew of the merchant vessel, Pelot brought both ships into Beaufort. Elliott and his "marines" shared in the prize money when the *A.B. Thompson* was later sold. The crew of the unlucky merchantman was held by the Confederate government through the summer before being exchanged for Southern civilians being held captive by U.S. authorities, who repeatedly called the seizure of the *A.B. Thompson* an act of piracy.[9]

A decision was made to protect Port Royal Sound by establishing earthwork forts on both sides of the entrance. General P.G.T. Beauregard was not in favor of this idea, as the forts could not provide mutual support across the two-mile-wide channel. But he submitted under pressure from South Carolina's new governor, Francis Pickens. Initially, little was done to

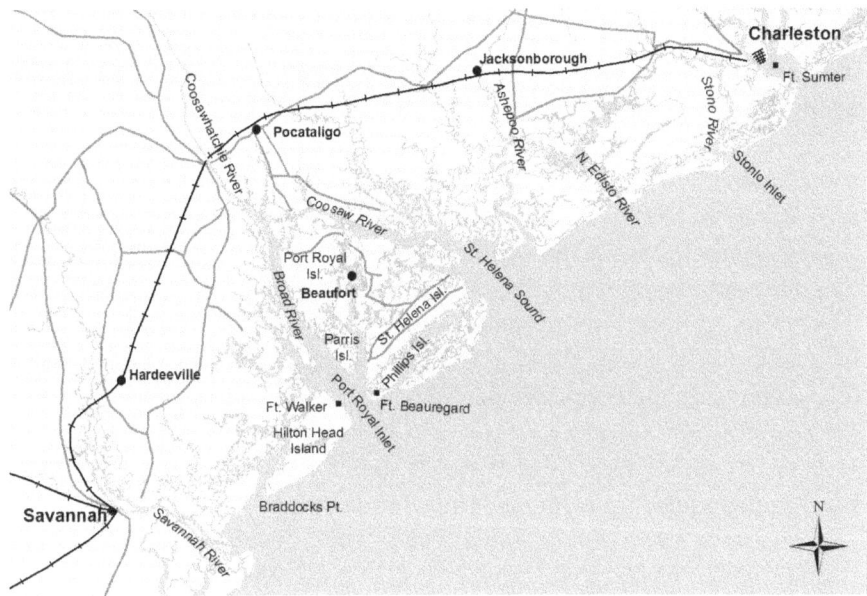

Map of South Carolina's Lowcountry in 1860. *Courtesy of Scott Williams and the Chesterfield Historical Society of Virginia.*

carry out the work, because the prevailing thinking was that the war would be decided in a single battle and events in Virginia were setting the stage. The first Battle of Manassas occurred on July 21 and resulted in a resounding Confederate victory. The South was exuberant but soon came to terms with the realization that the war would be continued. With that mindset, efforts to erect the forts—Fort Beauregard at Bay Point to the north of the sound and Fort Walker on Hilton Head Island to the south—surged then ebbed several times as the military department in which Beaufort fell went through a series of changes in command. By the end of October, the forts were serviceable but incomplete and measured at being two and five-eighths miles apart.[10] Few of the heavy, long-range cannon needed were provided, and the smaller guns supplementing them did not meet the demands for which the forts were planned. Captain Elliott and his company were assigned with one other artillery company to garrison Fort Beauregard, with Elliott as fort commander. Support in the form of infantry was available to assist in protecting against any enemy landings.

At the start of the war, Union leaders determined that a blockade of Southern ports was a necessity. At the same time, it was recognized that establishment of supporting bases for the blockading ships was a prerequisite.

These bases would be used for the supply, repair and maintenance of blockading vessels as well as serving as a point from which to carry out land operations by the army against the Confederacy. The navy carried out a significant study of potential sites along the South Atlantic coast and, in July, issued a lengthy report weighing the benefits and drawbacks and concerns for each to Secretary of the Navy Gideon Welles. Three potential sites were thoroughly considered and analyzed. Bull's Bay, north of Charleston, was declared the preferred choice, followed closely by St. Helena Sound. These sites were favored because of their remote environments and ease in ensuring security against Confederate threats. Port Royal, for a number of reasons, was the least-desirable selection. One particular paragraph in the report stands out in presenting a contrast between Port Royal and St. Helena: "Stephen Elliott, Jr. of Parry's Island, a nephew of George P. Elliott, has been employed in fortifying Port Royal, *every foot of which he is familiar with*, while not a planter knows Saint Helena."[11] This astounding statement attests to Elliott's widespread reputation of intimate familiarity with the area. Presenting him as a potential threat and alluding to the fact that Port Royal was being fortified were just two of several factors in relegating Port Royal to least-desirable status. However, views eventually changed over the following months, with Port Royal rising to the top of the list and becoming the target.

In late October, an armada of warships, along with numerous transports carrying supplies, equipment and troops for an amphibious assault, departed Hampton Roads, Virginia, destined to Port Royal. The fleet was battered by a powerful storm, and not all of the vessels rendezvoused off the sound on November 3. Noticeably missing were ships carrying ammunition, ordnance and landing craft for the army. Nevertheless, on November 7, the Union navy went forward with the plan to bombard Forts Walker and Beauregard into submission, thereby removing the major obstacles to their plan.

Confederate forces, aware of the armada's presence since its arrival, were prepared as best as possible, but calls for additional infantry support had not yet been fulfilled. Captain Elliott and his command had trained hard with their guns over the previous months and were likely now facing their first battle with much trepidation, as it was a direct threat to their homes and families. Colonel R.G.M. Dunovant, senior officer at Bay Point, with six companies of his Twelfth South Carolina Infantry present to support Fort Beauregard, tasked Elliott with ensuring that an escape route was available to avoid capture if the situation called for it. Through his father, who was present and serving as chaplain for the post, Elliott asked for flatboats to be pre-positioned at a site on St. Helena Island far

1861 sketch of Fort Beauregard on Bay Point at entrance of Port Royal Sound. *Library of Congress.*

away from any enemy guns or other immediate threats and planned a tentative route back to the mainland.[12]

The Battle of Port Royal Sound began about 9:30 on the morning of November 7, and Beauregard's reservations about the forts were immediately apparent. Initially firing on both forts, the Union warships quickly wheeled left to concentrate their firepower on Fort Walker. Shortly after, several vessels moved closer and to a position allowing them to enfilade the fort's flank. Raked by the crossfire of the armada's heavy guns, the defenders fought with spirit for nearly five hours until it became apparent that the situation was hopeless. With most of the guns knocked out of action and little powder remaining, orders were given to evacuate the fort.

Elliott and his garrison had watched the events at Fort Walker with concern. His garrison fired its long-range guns at the enemy ships with little apparent success, as they, more often than not, were out of range. Still, one gun fired fifty-seven shots and another slightly fewer. A third exploded on its thirty-second shot, wounding seven, including Elliott. In his after-action report, Elliott wrote in part, "The flagship was supposed to be on fire twice. Our fire was directed almost exclusively at the larger vessels. They were seen to be struck repeatedly, but the great distance—never less than 2,500 yards—prevented our ascertaining the extent of injury."[13] The fort did indeed receive some accurate and severe shelling from the ships, but damage was not extensive and caused no casualties.

Shortly after 2:00 p.m., Colonel Dunovant sought Elliott in the fort and inquired about the situation at Fort Walker. Elliott replied, "Fort Walker has been silenced, Sir." Dunovant then asked, "By what do you judge?" Elliott's response was one of keen observation and a model of brevity. "By the facts that the fort has been subjected to a heavy enfilade and direct fire to which it has ceased to reply; that, the vessels having terminated their fire, the flagship has steamed up and fired a single shot, which was unanswered, and thereupon cheering was heard from the fleet."[14]

Dunovant concurred and, realizing his small force would not be able to withstand a sustained bombardment and assault, gave orders to prepare for evacuation while retreat was still possible. An hour later, Fort Beauregard was abandoned, to be occupied by the Union forces the next day.[15] Leaving Bay Point, the weary Confederates, grateful for Elliott's contingency plan, took a circuitous route before reaching the mainland at Port Royal Ferry. Beaufort and the surrounding islands were now open to Union control, and the white residents fled the area that night, many leaving their slaves behind. The loss of the forts meant that the Union

Wartime image of Fort Beauregard at Bay Point. *Library of Congress.*

navy and army had secured a fine base to utilize for future operations. It was a staggering blow to the South, one that would result in a continued threat to the Charleston and Savannah Railroad, a vital link connecting the two cities. Port Royal Sound would soon be the base of operations for the Union South Atlantic Blockading Squadron and a major base of operations for the blue-coated army.

The new commander of the Department of South Carolina, Georgia and East Florida, Major General Robert E. Lee, arrived in Charleston the day of the battle and set up his headquarters at Pocotaligo after assuming command the next day.[16] Orders were quickly issued to establish defensive positions away from the shoreline and inland at key points where the terrain favored the defenders while, at the same time, presenting a hindrance to any enemy land movement from Port Royal Sound. Infantry and artillery commands were strategically placed to respond to any threat, with the largest concentrations stationed at Pocotaligo, Hardeeville and Garden's Corner. Earthworks were soon prepared at key positions such as Bluffton, Port Royal Ferry, Honey Hill and elsewhere; they would prove to be invaluable to the Confederacy in containing future enemy movements. The overriding goal was to prevent the enemy from severing the Charleston and Savannah Railroad.

After-action reports of the Battle of Port Royal Sound were prepared and submitted by the various unit commanders. Colonel Dunovant mentioned Elliott in a glowing manner.

> *I cannot close this report without drawing special attention to the high qualities of the officer exhibited by Captain Elliott, commanding that work. Compelled from the necessities of our position to act the part of engineer, ordnance officer, and commander of the fort, he exhibited an energy and intelligence in preparing the batteries for the fight which were only equaled by the gallantry and firmness of the defense.*[17]

Brigadier General Thomas Drayton, overall Confederate commander in the action, was even more lavish in praise of Captain Elliott:

> *But among the many officers and men honorably noticed...none of them are so justly entitled to well-merited encomium as Capt. Stephen Elliott, the commander of the fort. Others may have exhibited an equal amount of cool bravery in front of the foe, but his opportunities enabled him to surpass all other brother officers in the skillful arrangement of his defenses, superb*

*condition of his batteries, and the high discipline which he had imparted to his model company* [Beaufort Volunteer Artillery], *the creature of his own indefatigable exertions.*[18]

Such high praise was certainly bound to attract notice of Elliott's capabilities, leadership and organizational skills. One of those taking notice was Robert E. Lee, with whom Elliott was in occasional personal contact over the next few months. These reports document that he possessed the necessary attributes for higher command, and he would eventually be promoted to handle substantially more responsibility.

THE VICTORIOUS UNION FORCES moved fairly slowly in consolidating their gains. A South Carolina newspaper account summarized their efforts in a concise manner:

*The movements of the enemy have been extremely cautious; exploring and pillaging unguarded points on Hilton Head Island, Pinckney Island and Port Royal Island; sounding Broad River about eighteen miles up, under range of their gun-boats always; seizing a few negro men for labor, leaving the rest; gathering a small quantity of...cotton; and lastly, raking in such quantities of provisions as have not been burned.*[19]

With the fall of Beaufort and surrounding islands, vast quantities of valuable cotton had been left behind, susceptible to seizure by Union forces. The cotton, mostly already picked and baled, would be a lucrative prize for Northern interests. Realizing it was only a matter of time before the Union would secure it, Brigadier General R.S. Ripley, commander of provisional forces in the Department of South Carolina, issued orders on November 16 for four or more parties of volunteers to return to the Port Royal Sound area and, among other things, "prevent the enemy from getting possession of the cotton." Destruction of any cotton found was authorized if it could not be removed.[20]

One of these volunteer parties was led by Stephen Elliott. For a week, he and thirty of his men made a full reconnaissance of Port Royal Island and its vicinity. Finding it deserted but for former slaves, they carried out their assigned mission and burned thirteen cotton houses containing more than five hundred bales—all the cotton remaining on the island. Elliott, with a few others, then crossed to Parris Island in a small boat and set fire to an unpicked cotton crop having the equivalent of about seventy bales. Feeling relatively safe but alert to any enemy movements toward them, men were allowed to visit their homes around Beaufort before returning to Hendersonville on the mainland on December 5.[21]

On his return, Elliott immediately wrote a letter to Charlotte, who had taken the children to safety farther inland. His first words in the letter were, "I send to my darling wife a sprig of geranium I picked from her bush in Beaufort on Wednesday night." He then mentioned the reconnaissance and noted that each man was allowed to visit his home. "Nothing was left in ours except stair mats and oilcloths and odds and ends."[22] He wrote without rancor or malice and in a manner certainly intended to ease the grief he knew Charlotte would feel. Whether the looting and pillaging were carried out by Union troops or by former slaves was never mentioned, but whatever personal treasures, mementos and keepsakes the family had were now gone. There was little joy in Christmas 1861.

## 3
# YEAR OF TRANSITION (1862)

Union forces proceeded methodically in consolidating their gains after the Battle of Port Royal Sound, and as more men, equipment and supplies arrived, the process of establishing the facilities for the fleet and the army post began. Confederate forces continued development of their interior defensive positions and watched as occasional forays by Union troops, supported by gunboats, occurred along the waterways. The blockade of Charleston, begun the previous May, began to grow tighter as facilities allowing for supply and repairs for blockading vessels were enhanced at Port Royal Sound.

On March 3, General Robert E. Lee was recalled to Richmond by President Jefferson Davis.[23] His work along the coast would be a lasting legacy. Lee's foresight and strong hand, while ruffling the feathers of some, set the stage for successful defense against numerous Union attempts to break the railroad, interrupt vital communications and traffic between Charleston and Savannah and threaten each of those cities as the war surged on. He also left the army at Pocotaligo in the capable hands of Colonel William S. Walker, who had arrived as a captain and staff officer with Lee in November. In December, Lee was so impressed with Walker's abilities that he requested Walker be promoted to colonel of cavalry. In February, the promotion was authorized.[24]

The spring brought forth the first of the "great battles," at Shiloh, Tennessee. There, in a massive engagement over two days (April 6 and 7), the horrors of warfare were first brought to light, shocking both the

North and the South with incredibly large numbers of casualties. Almost simultaneously, Union general George B. McClellan began his Peninsula Campaign by moving his huge army toward Richmond. All eyes were directed toward Richmond as McClellan inched forward, delayed by occasional engagements, to within about five miles of the city. Certainly, Stephen Elliott was concerned about his brothers Ralph and William, for their regiment was in the thick of things in Virginia. The situation in the Lowcountry of South Carolina was serious and threatening, but the region was a quiet backwater compared to other areas.

The first serious Union attempt to sever the railroad between Charleston and Savannah occurred in late May. A sizeable detachment of infantry supported by cavalry and artillery, perhaps one thousand men in all, left Beaufort about 9:30 on the evening of May 28 bent on cutting the railroad at Pocotaligo near Yemasee. Reaching the Port Royal Ferry site around daybreak the next morning, the entire command was on the mainland by 8:00 a.m. Confederate cavalry pickets detected the move and, after skirmishing briefly, retired to carry the news to Colonel Walker, now commander of the Third Military District. He immediately informed senior officers in Charleston and Savannah of this new threat and issued calls for reinforcements.

Five small companies of cavalry, about 125 men total, were all that stood between the attackers and the railroad. Skirmishers were sent forward to stall the enemy advance. Three different times they stood their ground until forced from their position, only to re-form a short distance away and challenge the approaching force again. Badly outnumbered and lacking artillery and infantry support, the stalwart cavalrymen were determined to hold the enemy at bay until reinforcements could arrive. One company armed only with revolvers was held in reserve, with another acting as horse holders. The other three, a total of 76 men, used the woods, canals and ditches to their advantage in contesting the Union advance. Armed mainly with shotguns, they opened fire on the enemy advance guard at a range of forty yards. From this point on, the action became more widespread. This small but determined force kept the Union advance in check from 10:30 a.m. to 1:30 p.m., when the Yankees managed to flank them with a force of about 300 men. Retiring to a stronger position within a mile of the railroad and receiving additional ammunition, the defenders awaited a continuation of the action.

Unbeknownst to them, the Union field commander decided to retreat at about 2:30 p.m. Much of the planned movement had turned into a debacle for the Yankees. Cavalry and artillery were delayed nearly every step of the

Wartime photo showing Union pickets at the Port Royal Ferry dock on the Coosaw River, with the mainland in the background. *Library of Congress.*

way, and while some of the force saw no action at all, the portion that did was nearly out of ammunition. Confederates were relieved to see Captain Elliott arrive with three pieces of his artillery along with two companies of infantry at about 4:00 p.m. Shortly afterward, word was received that the enemy was in the process of retiring. Pursuit lasted until late that evening without further contact, and the entire Union force was off the mainland by 3:00 a.m. the next morning. Though substantial quantities of ammunition were expended, casualties were quite light, at less than a dozen on each side.[25]

One Union colonel grossly overestimated the small Confederate force opposing him, stating in his after-action report: "It is…difficult to state the force of the enemy, but it could not have been less than 600 to 800. There were six companies of mounted riflemen, besides infantry, among which were a considerable number of colored men."[26] The determination of the small force of dismounted cavalrymen involved saved the day and prevented disaster.

The next morning, Confederate troops continued their march. Colonel Walker wrote that, on reaching Port Royal Ferry, "Capt. Stephen Elliott Jr., brought up his artillery and battered the ferry-house, which sheltered their pickets, and their flat-boats, with which they had effected a crossing, at a range of 250 yards."[27]

THE JOY OF THIS victory was sweet but quickly forgotten because of other events happening within a two-day span. The Battle of Seven Pines (May 31–June 1), an all-out effort to drive McClellan and his huge army from the gates of Richmond, though producing heavy casualties on each side, failed. The most important result was that Confederate general Joseph Johnston was severely wounded and replaced by Robert E. Lee. Another event, much closer to home, occurred when a large flotilla left Beaufort on June 1 with several thousand soldiers under orders to disembark on both James Island and Johns Island, a move threatening Charleston with land attack. Times were looking bleak again, but the Confederate victory at the Battle of Secessionville on the outskirts of Charleston two weeks later revived the lagging spirits.

On the night of June 6, Elliott led another small-unit raid. With twenty men of the Beaufort Volunteer Artillery and a cannon supported by fifty-five riflemen, he crossed the river at Port Royal Ferry to the enemy position used in the raid a week earlier. Union pickets heard his boat approaching in darkness. A newspaper report reads, "Here he was hailed and replied in negro lingo so well intoned as to deceive the Yankees until he could see their white faces, when, by signal, a volley was poured into them."[28] Landing their boats, they set fire to the ferry-house and commenced to destroy the flatboats and other craft at the location before retiring. Colonel W.S. Walker's short but concise report of the raid read in part: "I am indebted to Capt. Stephen Elliott, who is a sailor as well as a soldier, for the efficient organization of the expedition. He exhibited coolness, adroitness, and resolution in successfully carrying out his plans. A few rounds of spherical cases were fired to sweep the causeway while the flats were being towed off, which had the effect of rousing the whole island."[29]

June 11 was a signal day for Stephen Elliott. His brother Middleton Stuart Elliott, who was one of twelve cadets graduated from The Citadel in April, enlisted in the Beaufort Volunteer Artillery as a private.[30] Separated in age by eleven years, the two brothers must have had a joyful reunion and taken time to get caught up on each other's wartime experiences. No doubt they would have had brothers William and Ralph in their thoughts. William's company converted from infantry to light artillery earlier in the year but was still in Virginia. Ralph was soon to be promoted to first lieutenant of his company. He, like William, remained at his post in Virginia, now serving under General Robert E. Lee in his newly named Army of Northern Virginia.

DESPITE BEING SHELLED ON May 31 and set afire on June 6, the Port Royal ferry-house still stood and remained a favorite spot for Union sharpshooters harassing Confederate pickets on the mainland. Colonel Walker arranged for a small raiding force to complete the destruction of this building, and again Captain Elliott was in the forefront. In a raid lasting just thirty minutes on July 4, under the covering fire of two guns of the Beaufort Volunteer Artillery driving in the enemy pickets, Elliott and a dozen men crossed the Coosaw River with a barrel of turpentine, entered the building and set it afire. With it engulfed in flames, the raiding party returned and watched the destruction from the mainland. Walker's report, in part, read, "All the movements were marked with coolness and precision."[31]

August would prove to be a memorable month for Elliott. Though still a captain, he was named commander of all artillery in the Third Military District. This was a huge responsibility for a mere captain, for there were enough unassigned batteries in the district to have formed a battalion requiring command by a lieutenant colonel. With this change, Elliott's brother-in-law Lieutenant Henry Middleton Stuart assumed nominal command of the Beaufort Volunteer Artillery. With his battery carrying the reputation of a superb and finely tuned unit, this additional duty was likely intended to allow Elliott to exert a positive influence on other batteries, thereby increasing their proficiency.

In this same month, Colonel Walker saw an opportunity to strike the enemy in a manner far harder than in previous months. Aside from the Port Royal ferry-house raids, most other strikes had been against small, lightly manned picket posts. However, information gathered from three Union deserters and a daring reconnaissance carried out by two prominent officers with local ties opened up the possibility of a more significant raid against an enemy post stationed on Pinckney Island, an island on Port Royal Sound sandwiched between Hilton Head Island and the mainland near Bluffton. The reconnaissance details presented by Lieutenant Colonel Charles J. Colcock, Second Battalion South Carolina Cavalry, and Captain John H. Mickler, Eleventh South Carolina Infantry, suggested that the enemy position on the northeastern point of the island was vulnerable, though an attempted raid would be fraught with danger. Their information matched that provided by the Union deserters. The size of the post might be as many as one hundred men, gunboats were often in the vicinity and large enemy forces were close by. However, duty there was routine, and security was generally in a relaxed state. Colonel Walker envisioned a raiding party in sufficient strength, using darkness and the element of surprise, to capture the entire garrison and then depart as quickly as it arrived. Summoning Captains Elliott and Mickler to his headquarters, he tasked them with devising a plan for such a mission.[32]

Elliott and Mickler shared many similarities. Each was bold, intelligent, courageous and highly knowledgeable of the area. The intrepid pair set out together on August 18 for a final reconnaissance of Pinckney Island and, on returning, confirmed to Colonel Walker that a raid was feasible. Walker immediately appointed Elliott as commander of the expedition and left the pair to develop a detailed plan. Elliott wasted no time in preparing for the expedition, and orders were issued that very day. Captain Mickler was to have one hundred men and four boats ready on August 21. Elliott called for fifty men from his artillery battery armed with muskets and a boat with a small cannon plus five other boats. The two parties rendezvoused as planned, and at 3:00 a.m. on August 21, the combined companies departed in darkness for the ten-mile trip, timed to land prior to dawn.[33] Elliott's knowledge of the island, tides and currents in the channel was key to landing in the right place at the right time.

Execution of the plan went almost precisely as drawn up. The boats reached the selected landing area undetected, and the men, well-briefed beforehand, quickly followed their officers across open ground to the cover of foliage on one side of the camp. Then, with complete surprise, they made their presence known. Some pickets fired on them, resulting in a brief and one-sided shoot-out, with fifteen Union soldiers killed and thirty-six others (including four wounded) captured. Of the fifty-seven Yankees present that morning, just six escaped. Confederate casualties totaled eight men wounded, but just two by enemy fire. The other casualties were from friendly fire brought on partly by the early morning darkness. Prisoners were hastily moved to the boats, where they and their captors began the return trip to safety. Elliott reported that he and his men, as per orders, did not linger at the Union camp. Taking only company records and two boats, they departed the island a mere fifteen minutes after landing.[34]

Colonel Walker was ecstatic with the results. This dangerous raid by brave men and officers was by all accounts a smashing success. In his report to General Pemberton, commanding the Department of South Carolina and Georgia, Walker wrote in part: "I knew that the high qualities of the leaders and their men would secure the prompt execution, and the result has amply justified my confidence....I must specially mention the conspicuous gallantry of Captains Elliott and Mickler." Later, he gave great praise to Elliott when referencing his previous raids: "I have been indebted to Capt. Stephen Elliott, who is a sailor as well as a soldier, for the organization and largely for the execution of these affairs. With great zeal and enterprise he has contributed a sagacity and prudence which have invariably secured success."[35]

Elliott graciously shared credit for success with Mickler by including the following in his official report. "It is a just tribute to a gallant officer to say that Captain Mickler, by his ceaseless energy and labor for days and nights previously, as well as by his valuable suggestions, contributed in no small degree to the success of the enterprise, while by his impetuous courage he rendered complete the surprise of the enemy."[36]

By any standard, the raid was successful and removed any doubts that the small Confederate force in the Lowcountry was aggressive and possessed daring leaders and brave men capable of brilliant feats. Captain Mickler and Lieutenant Colonel Colcock would prove themselves multiple times before the war's end.

SEPTEMBER TURNED TRAGIC FOR Stephen and Charlotte, however. Their eldest son, Stephen Habersham Elliott, died on September 8 at age six in McPhersonville, a small town about ten miles northwest of Port Royal Ferry, where the family had found refuge.[37] Having lost their home and most of their personal possessions, their son's death was a painful reminder of how much had changed in less than a year.

Middleton Elliott was detached from the Beaufort Volunteer Artillery on September 22 and assigned to the engineers as a surveyor. Stephen was likely happy to see his youngest brother removed from harm's way. He also was probably anxious about William and Ralph. Three major battles had taken place since Robert E. Lee had taken command of the Army of Northern Virginia. The Seven Days Battles (June 25–July 1) drove McClellan away from Richmond; Second Manassas (August 28–30) opened the door to taking the war to the north. That dream was shattered at Sharpsburg on September 22, and Lee's army returned to Virginia.

OCTOBER WAS A DIFFERENT month, and the first week brought great news. Colonel Walker recommended Stephen Elliott Jr. to become the new commander of the Eleventh South Carolina Infantry. General Beauregard, now the senior officer in South Carolina, having succeeded General Pemberton in September, replied to Walker on October 5: "Your recommendation of Capt. Stephen Elliott to succeed Colonel Ellis, Eleventh South Carolina Volunteers, has just been received and will be forwarded to the War Department, approved of by me of course, but the result is quite doubtful."[38] It was obvious Walker thought highly of Elliott and wanted to do all within his power to have him promoted. This was Beauregard's introduction to Elliott, a man he would come to know very well in the next year.

The Union commander in Beaufort had not been sitting idly, though. Scouts and spies had been active on the mainland identifying Confederate positions, mapping potential routes to the railroad and securing as much vital information as possible in anticipation of a strike to sever the railroad. Possible troop landing sites were explored, with tributaries charted and sounded, to determine where there was enough depth for their transports and gunboats.

In the late hours of October 21, a force of forty-five hundred men, mostly infantry but with some artillery and cavalry, were loaded aboard a number of transports and flatboats supported by gunboats and set sail toward the mouth of the Pocataligo River for the explicit purpose of conducting a one-day, two-pronged raid. The goal was to sever the Charleston and Savannah Railroad at Pocataligo about eight miles away from the main force landing site. The main force was to march toward Pocataligo, while the second prong went up the Coosawhatchie River before disembarking, to threaten the railroad facilities at the village of Coosawhatchie. Plans went awry when a transport ran aground, causing a delay of almost four hours, time valuable to the defenders. Confederate scouts issued a warning of the landing and Colonel Walker placed a

Wartime sketch of railroad depot at Pocotaligo, South Carolina, on the Charleston and Savannah Railroad. *Library of Congress.*

call for reinforcements from Charleston and Savannah. The main Union force proceeded rapidly for about four miles when it met the first line of Confederate resistance.[39]

Colonel Walker's command was spread over sixty miles, and recalls were sent for immediate concentration at Pocotaligo. Until reinforcements arrived, Walker had twelve pieces of artillery under the overall command of Stephen Elliott, a couple of infantry companies and several small companies of cavalry for a total of 475 men of all arms. However, discounting the cavalry's horse holders, only 405 men were present to meet the Yankees.[40] The artillery, consisting of four guns of the Beaufort Volunteer Artillery and eight from the Nelson Light Artillery, was to play a major role in the upcoming battle.

Walker placed two guns of the Beaufort Volunteer Artillery in a prepared position guarding the approach route used by the enemy and supported it with sharpshooters and two companies of cavalry acting as skirmishers. When the enemy came in sight about 11:30 a.m., the two cannon opened fire. With their forward progress stopped, the Union infantry deployed in line of battle, uncertain of how many Confederates were to their front. Heavy skirmishing began. The Yankees brought up their own artillery, and the engagement became rather heavy. At this point, the Confederates began an orderly withdrawal. Having delayed the enemy nearly an hour, the small force began falling back to another position, destroying the small bridges on the route after crossing them, adding further delay to the renewed Yankee advance.

After advancing another mile and a half, the leading Yankee elements were fired on by several pieces of Elliott's artillery posted in advantageous positions covering the road near a causeway over the swampy ground. Again, the Yankees had to deploy. With the infantry stymied again, Union artillery was brought up and, along with heavy musketry, engaged Walker's skirmishers for forty-five minutes in a savage exchange of fire. Elliott's guns, firing canister and shell, inflicted substantial casualties on the Yankees and twice drove them away. Still, the heavy fire from the enemy's rifled muskets brought down a number of the cannon crews and their horses. Walker finally gave orders to withdraw a little over two miles to positions at another causeway. Destroying bridges as they crossed them, Walker's men reached the position and awaited the enemy arrival.

For the third time that day, the Yankees found themselves facing Confederate defensive positions protected by swamp and marsh. Still, they immediately deployed and initiated a general engagement with heavy musketry and artillery fire. Though causing heavy casualties to the Confederate cannon crews, their own casualties mounted quickly. After two long hours of intense firing, just three Confederate cannon (two of them from the Beaufort Volunteer Artillery) were still in operation but remained in the fray, throwing projectiles of all sorts and helping to keep the enemy at bay. About 4:30 p.m., Walker received a fresh battalion of two hundred riflemen that was immediately placed in line, relieving some of the pressure and causing great concern to the enemy.[41]

With night approaching, ammunition running low and Confederate reinforcements arriving, it was obvious that the intended goal of the Union force to cut the railroad was unobtainable. About 6:00 p.m., orders were reluctantly given by the Union commander to withdraw and return to the ships.

The second Union force made its way undetected almost to the village of Coosawhatchie and came close enough to fire on a train bringing Confederate reinforcements. Unfortunately for them, the Confederates already in place there, along with the reinforcements, presented too strong a defense for further action. A withdrawal was commenced right away.

Confederate casualties altogether tallied 168, while the Yankees suffered 340.[42] The Battle of Pocotaligo was a stunning victory for the small, hard-pressed Confederate force and a stinging disappointment to its much larger, more well-equipped foe. Elliott's artillery played a major role in the victory. Union general John Brannan wrote of it in his after-action report.

> [T]*he rebels threw a most terrific fire of grape, shot, shell, canister, and musket balls, killing and wounding great numbers of my command....* [T]*he infantry were twice driven out of the woods with great slaughter by the overwhelming fire of the enemy, whose missiles tore through the woods like hail....* [At his final position] *the rebels opened a murderous fire upon us from batteries of siege guns and field pieces on the farther side of the creek. Our skirmishers advanced and, with what cover they could obtain...did considerable execution among the enemy.*[43]

Colonel Walker's after-action report was most generous in praise. There was much heroism from those involved, and he took special efforts to mention the names of specific commands and men who had withstood the advance of an enemy ten times their strength. It was certainly merited. Confederate artillery had remained at the forefront all day long despite incurring heavy losses. Walker mentioned the Beaufort Volunteer Artillery and Elliott: "The Beaufort Volunteer Artillery fought with great courage and their pieces were admirably served. Captain Stephen Elliott, whose name is identified with the history of this coast by many a daring exploit, behaved with his accustomed coolness, skill, and determination."[44] Elliott's judicious use of his artillery was apparent to all. He placed it skillfully and used it effectively. Surrounded by deep forests and swampy areas, there was little room to maneuver in the various actions throughout the day. Still, Elliott and his well-trained gun crews deserve great credit for their part in delaying the enemy long enough for reinforcements to arrive while, at the same time, inflicting substantial casualties on the blue-coated foe.

Walker himself deserved much credit for the Confederate victory by his inspiring leadership, foresight and skill in placing troops in advantageous positions. Receiving Walker's after-action report, General Beauregard forwarded news of the victory to the War Department in Richmond. Showing a full understanding and appreciation of what had transpired, Beauregard recommended that Walker be promoted. The satisfaction of this signal victory resounded across South Carolina, giving renewed confidence to its citizens. A letter urging promotion for Colonel Walker, signed by nine leading citizens of Charleston, was sent to the secretary of war on October 30. It read in part: "The people of the state believe that, under the rule of a Merciful Providence, we are indebted for this brilliant victory, to the skill of Col. W.S. Walker....[W]e therefore pray that such promotion be awarded Col. Walker for his eminent service to our city and our country."[45] The War Department, to its credit, also recognized Walker's diligence and efficient leadership role in the victory and, in just a few days, authorized Walker's promotion to brigadier general. Walker received another honor. Unofficial, but coming from the men he commanded in this battle, it was a mark of honor and respect by those under his command that day. He became referred to by his troops as "Live Oak," a nickname bestowed on him "for the gallant fight he gave the Federals at a point of oaks near Pocotaligo."[46]

On November 15, Walker wrote a letter to the adjutant and inspector of the Confederate army in Richmond, General Samuel Cooper, again recommending Elliott for promotion, this time adding Elliott's heroism and skill in directing the artillery at Pocotaligo. The primary justifications for promotion were given in a very concise manner. "He passed the Board of Examiners as highly proficient. He was distinguished at Bay Point [Battle of Port Royal] and highly distinguished in the late skirmish at Yemassee and Battle of Pocotaligo. His partisan exploits have been frequent, daring and resourceful."[47]

General Walker wrote another letter to Cooper on November 21. This one recommended Reverend Stephen Elliott Sr. as an army chaplain. "Mr. Elliott is known to many of the troops of my command and his preaching has proven acceptable to them. After the Battle of Pocotaligo he remained several days in the hospital administering to the wounded and dying." The reverend's appointment as chaplain of Walker's command was confirmed on December 12.[48]

In December, the Beaufort Volunteer Artillery received a brand-new battery of cannon. A newspaper article heralded this news: "Capt. Stephen Elliott's command has recently been furnished with a full battery of six brass guns complete with accoutrements. The iron battery of five guns...which the Yankees pronounced 'so terrible' 22nd October last, at Pocataligo, have been transferred to...[the] Palmetto Light Artillery."[49]

The year 1862 soon came to a close laden with optimism. A major battle at Fredericksburg, Virginia, in mid-December resulted in a smashing Southern victory, raising spirits across the South. Stephen's high spirits were likely dampened by concern about his brother Ralph, who was severely wounded in the battle and would spend nearly three months recuperating in a Richmond army hospital.

## 4

# CHANGES ABOUND (JANUARY–AUGUST 1863)

In January, General Walker still faced a problem that many commanders encountered. The colonelcy of the Eleventh South Carolina was vacant, and he felt the regiment's lieutenant colonel was not competent enough to be elevated to such a command position. In his mind, the best man to lead the regiment was Captain Stephen Elliott Jr. However, his November letter to Samuel Cooper in Richmond recommending Elliott for promotion to colonel of the regiment remained unanswered. There were complications, because the Beaufort Volunteer Artillery, formerly Company A of the regiment, had been reorganized in March 1862 as an independent command of light artillery. Some thought this was just a technicality, but to the army, it was much more. The matter remained unaddressed for several months, at least partly because of the complications such promotion would involve. On April 21, Walker wrote a follow-up letter to Adjutant and Inspector General Cooper advising that he had heard nothing regarding his November 15 letter recommending promotion for Elliott. In it, he gave more detailed justification for his recommendation. Citing Elliott's success in the raid in Pinckney Island and the display of his personal valor and skill while directing artillery at Pocotaligo, he concluded with a heartfelt appeal:

> In the earlier history of the war he earned the reputation as a daring scout. Within the last year he has made several attacks in boats upon the enemy's pickets with more or less success without loss to himself. These partisan activities have the effect of changing the attitude of the enemy from offensive

*to the defensive.... The executive has the opportunity of placing in its proper position an officer who has demonstrated his fitness for command and I would earnestly recommend it. I request it as indispensable to the* [present army] *reorganization.*[50]

Unbeknownst to Walker, the matter reached General Robert E. Lee before his follow-up letter, indicating the War Department was torn as to what avenues could be taken. Lee, who had worked closely with Walker and thought highly enough of him when in South Carolina to recommend him for promotion from captain to colonel of cavalry, took time from his busy schedule and other demands to compose a letter to the secretary of war on April 10. Stating that while he was concerned such promotion could be authorized under army regulations, he backed promotion for Elliott and wrote in part:

*When in command of that department in winter of '61 & '62, I had a good opportunity of forming an estimate on the qualifications of Capt. Elliott and considered him one of the best officers in the department. I selected him on several occasions for the performance of special duty, in which he showed good judgement, and exhibited intelligence, boldness and sagacity. I do not know that a better man can be found to fill the Colonelcy of the 11th Regt SCV provided he can be appointed and I write at any rate recommending him promotion as Lt. Col. Of Artillery should there be a vacancy in that arm of the service."*[51]

This resounding endorsement from Lee cleared most of the obstacles facing the War Department and, on April 30, Elliott received promotion to major of artillery. This opened the way for his brother-in-law Henry M. Stuart to be promoted to captain and permanently in command of the Beaufort Volunteer Artillery.

April was indeed a banner month for Stephen Elliott. On the ninth, he became involved in one of his most memorable deeds of the war. Early that morning, scouts reported that a Yankee gunboat, the *E.B. Hale*, was aground near Chisolm's Island and that an armed steamer, *George Washington*, was attempting to pull it off. General Walker alerted Elliott and ordered numerous commands out in hopes of destroying or capturing both vessels. Elliott, with the six guns of the Beaufort Volunteer Artillery and seven additional field pieces from other batteries in addition to a company of infantry, arrived about 4:00 a.m., just as the *Hale* was refloated and began moving toward Port Royal Ferry. Oddly, its consort did not join it but instead remained at anchorage. Under Walker's orders, some of the cannon were sent to intercept the *Hale* farther upstream if possible, while the remaining six guns were to monitor but not fire on the steamer about a mile away unless it started movement.

With daylight showing about 5:00 a.m., the *George Washington* was seen to begin moving. At that point, Confederate artillery commenced to fire and, with just two shots, secured an immediate hit, knocking out its rudder and steering while, at the same time, exploding its magazine, which set the ship afire. The ship immediately raised a white flag and began drifting to the other side of the channel, where the crew abandoned ship, leaving the vessel to sink in four feet of water and burn to near the waterline. Confederate gunners opened fire again on seeing the Union sailors fleeing across the marsh in violation of their white flag of surrender. Captain Elliott and a small party rowed to the smoking hulk where they found two men wounded and another one dead and sent them ashore. Shortly afterward, cries from other wounded Yankees were heard from the marsh, but before anything could be done about them, the *Hale* was seen returning. Not desiring an engagement with the gunboat but mindful of the wounded in the marsh, Elliott rowed toward the Union gunboat under a flag of truce and delivered the wounded and dead men taken off the *George Washington*. At the same time, he advised the ship's captain of those in the marsh and left. Two days later, he and a work party salvaged a twenty-four-pound howitzer and other equipment from the burnt vessel before enemy shelling from the opposite shore drove them away.

The sinking of a hated Yankee gunboat, especially one that had tormented them for months, was a source of gratification to Confederate forces in the area. General Walker again gave due recognition to those who had done so well. Among those mentioned were Elliott, about whom he wrote, "Capt. Stephen Elliott exhibited his characteristic coolness and skill as an artillery officer."[52] Unfortunately, events in Charleston overshadowed this exploit.

On April 7, the Union navy, with orders to take Charleston, took the first step by attempting to neutralize Fort Sumter at the harbor entrance. Collecting nine ironclads, seven monitors included, Admiral Samuel DuPont sortied up the main ship channel and, about 2:30 in the afternoon, began an ill-fated duel. For the next three hours, Fort Sumter showed its strength, absorbing the Union gunfire aimed at it while pounding the ships unmercifully with return fire. It was a one-sided battle, with Sumter receiving relatively minor damage but inflicting substantial damage to the ironclads.

One of them, the *Keokuk*, sank off Morris Island the next day, and five others were badly damaged. The battered ironclads simply proved to be no match for Sumter. This battle led the Yankees to later rethink their strategy on taking Fort Sumter and Charleston. For now, the joy of such a significant victory was welcomed in Charleston, throughout the state of South Carolina and all across the Confederacy. Stephen Elliott could never have imagined that this wondrous victory would soon affect him in a most dramatic and drastic manner.

No one could have known that the sinking of the *George Washington* was to be the last substantial action in the Beaufort area that Stephen Elliott would be involved in. On April 27, he was reported as "absent with leave on public duty by order of Gen'l Walker." In July, he reported to Charleston under orders for duty with siege and heavy artillery, where he worked with the Torpedo Department for a short while before being transferred to heavy artillery.[53] As a man of action, this sort of duty most likely was not what he was hoping for, but as he was a major of artillery with extensive ordnance and engineering background, the army placed him in an open billet needing his rank and experience.

July 1863 was a terrible month for the Confederacy. The momentum gained by the stunning victory at Chancellorsville, Virginia, in May was abruptly ended on July 4 by simultaneous disastrous defeats. In the East, Robert E. Lee's army was defeated at Gettysburg in a three-day battle with massive casualties on each side. In the West, almost thirty thousand Confederates surrendered at Vicksburg after a six-week siege. Stephen Elliott was likely quite anxious about his brothers. Ralph, elected captain of his company in the spring, survived the bloody carnage at Gettysburg, but William was one of those captured at Vicksburg. At the beginning of 1863, William had been promoted to captain and assigned to the staff of General Stephen Dill Lee as assistant adjutant general, a position he held until conclusion of the war in the Army of Tennessee. William's duties were purely administrative in nature, but he still distinguished himself in combat on two occasions in the Vicksburg Campaign. At Baker's Creek (Champion Hill), he picked up a fallen regimental flag and carried it through the raging battle, exposing himself to prolonged heavy fire while inspiring the men around him. At Vicksburg, a Union attack took some of the trench line but was driven back when he led a counterattack using twelve-pound cannon shells as grenades. William was promoted to major for his courage after being exchanged.[54] July 17 was likely a day that saddened Captain Elliott, for his fifteen-year-old half brother, Henry D. Elliott, enlisted as a private in the Beaufort Volunteer Artillery.[55]

FORT SUMTER WAS A name readily familiar to the average citizen of both the North and South since U.S. Army major Robert Anderson moved his command in a surreptitious manner from Fort Moultrie to Fort Sumter on December 26, 1860, just six days after South Carolina seceded from the Union. Sumter eventually became the site of the first shots of the War Between the States, marking Charleston as perhaps the most hated city in the South from the Northern perspective.

Sumter was one of many forts planned after the War of 1812 for protection of port cities along the U.S. Atlantic and Gulf Coasts. The first work began on it in early 1829, but for a variety of reasons, work was suspended several times. More than ten thousand tons of granite stone for the foundation were brought from Northern states and skillfully laid. Production of the millions of bricks needed was by nature slow and laborious. Seashells for the concrete, sand, bricks and other stones necessary for construction took time to be collected, produced and delivered. Occasional storms, the summer heat and yellow fever outbreaks caused further delays in erecting the fort.

Eventually, Fort Sumter took shape as a five-sided masonry edifice with three tiers for its planned complement of 135 cannon of various sizes. Slated to hold a garrison of nearly seven hundred men, it extended over nearly all of the approximate two and a half acres of the man-made island. In 1860, the fort was unfinished, as congressional funding was unavailable in 1858 and 1859, and it was equipped with just 60 heavy guns. It was not yet garrisoned, and the only troops in the vicinity throughout its construction were stationed at Fort Moultrie, just 1,700 yards away across the harbor channel. Sumter's size and appearance were awe-inspiring and certainly provided a sense of comfort and safety to the coastal citizens.

The Confederate bombardment in April 1861 resulted in some damage to the fort that was quickly repaired, and in 1863, Sumter was in good shape. However, events in April 1862 just one hundred miles to the south near Savannah captured attention of military circles around the world. Colonel Quincy Gillmore, a noted Union engineer, became enamored of a new type of gun originally designed for the navy: the heavy rifled cannon.

It fired a bullet-shaped shell weighing as much as three hundred pounds and packed with high explosives and was intended to penetrate its target, causing maximum damage. Cannon heretofore fired round projectiles with little penetrating power on a solid target. Despite a great deal of skepticism from others, Gillmore obtained authorization to employ several batteries of rifled cannon on Tybee Island against the Confederate stronghold at Fort Pulaski. After a punishing thirty-hour bombardment at long range, he forced surrender of the fort. With its brick walls breached and having no ordnance in its inventory with which to reply, there was no choice other than submission for the garrison. This long-range victory resulted in effectively sealing off the port of Savannah and brought Gillmore and the rifled cannon to the attention of Washington, D.C. It also marked the demise of masonry forts and defensive works across the world.

Engineers in Charleston were immediately aware, acutely so, of the vulnerability of Fort Sumter. After careful study and deliberation on how to best counter this new threat, certain steps were taken to enhance the fort's sustainability. Magazines were relocated to reduce chances of being hit by incoming projectiles. Cotton bales, along with filled sandbags by the thousands, were placed to buttress interior walls and reduce fragmentation risks from damage caused by shelling. Little could be done to protect the outer brick walls themselves, but imaginative efforts to ensure livability and safety of the garrison inside the fort's lower level were begun and continued until its abandonment in February 1865. Additionally, a number of valuable guns were removed and sent to other defensive positions protecting Charleston.

In July, Fort Sumter found itself in the crosshairs of a determined Union offensive intended to destroy its firepower capability and then occupy it, thus sealing Charleston's harbor entrance while opening up the seaward approaches for the outright capture of the city. The stunning defeat of the ironclads when trying to bombard Sumter into surrender the previous April led Washington's leaders to devise another plan to silence the fort. In May, Union leaders met in Washington to discuss plans for the capture of Charleston. The concept required close cooperation between the army and navy and was centered on Fort Sumter, seen as key to the effort to take the city. Fort Sumter had to be eliminated by the army under command of Quincy Gillmore, now a brigadier general as a result of his work at Fort Pulaski. Once Sumter was silenced, the fleet could pass quickly by other Confederate positions in the harbor straight to the city proper to unleash its huge guns at near-point-blank range, thus forcing abandonment and surrender of Charleston. To contribute to this grandiose plan, the army would land on the southern tip of Morris Island; move northward, driving Confederate forces away from their two positions at Batteries Wagner and Gregg; and eliminate the offensive power of Fort Sumter with devastating firepower from long range in conjunction with bombardment from the naval forces offshore. The only caveat was that, if circumstances called for it, Gillmore's army command might be reduced to meet reinforcement needs of Union armies elsewhere. No additional troops would be sent to Gillmore under any circumstances. This plan directly and specifically precluded any further attempts to take Charleston by land.[56]

On July 10, a massive Yankee force landed on the southern tip of Morris Island, overwhelming the small Confederate force there. Swiftly advancing three miles, the Yankees intended to take the last mile of the island the next day with an attack on Battery Wagner, a Confederate bastion across the narrowest part of the island, and then follow up with an assault on Battery Gregg on Cummings Point at the north end of the island. However, they were stopped cold at Battery Wagner with significant losses. Six days later, another all-out assault, preceded by a ten-hour bombardment of Wagner by Union artillery and naval ironclads, was launched and again repulsed with heavy casualties. The courageous stands by vastly outnumbered and outgunned Confederates caused a great deal of frustration to their blue-coated foes. General Gillmore, realizing his goal of quickly taking Morris Island was shattered, wrote, "Fort Sumter must be destroyed by guns placed as near it as to the site of Battery Wagner, and that every hour's delay in capturing that work permitted the enemy to strengthen his interior defenses, and thus render the entrance of our fleet more difficult."[57] When Gillmore began his advance on Morris Island, Beauregard and his engineers understood full well what his intentions were and what special threat he represented. Simply put, Sumter was in peril. The work to make contingencies in the fort's capability to withstand an expected severe pounding continued with extra effort and impetus while the fighting for Battery Wagner continued.

Resigned to the fact that direct assault was unworkable, Union engineers commenced building siege lines, inching ever closer to Battery Wagner on a daily basis. Building a series of parallels—trenches zigzagging across the beach with the excavated earth used to build berms protecting the attackers from Wagner's defensive fire—the Yankees proceeded slowly but steadily forward. Sumter's destruction, still the ultimate goal of the offensive, began with the establishment of numerous batteries with heavy rifled guns much sooner than originally planned. Firing over Battery Wagner on Sumter on August 12 from a range of two miles or more, far beyond the range of any

Wartime sketch of Fort Sumter being shelled by Union cannon on Morris Island in 1863. *Library of Congress.*

Confederate artillery, Union forces quickly found their target and prepared to commence a bombardment unlike any other previously seen. On August 17, the bombardment began in earnest, with almost one thousand shells fired at Sumter that day, followed by about five thousand more shots over the next few days.

On August 23, Yankee ironclads closed in, and Sumter showed that a limited defensive capability still remained by exchanging fire with them. Significantly, these were the fort's last shots of the war in a combat action. By the next day, the fort was in total shambles and just one of its forty guns was still serviceable, the others being dismounted or buried in rubble. On the night of September 1–2, Union ironclads subjected the fort to an intense five-hour bombardment, and Sumter, without means of defending itself, was finally considered by Union commanders as utterly destroyed, thus bringing what was termed the First Great Bombardment to a merciful end. In all, 7,305 huge projectiles, ranging from thirty to three hundred pounds, were hurled at Sumter in just sixteen days by Union artillery on Morris Island and the navy's monitors. The accuracy of the fire is evident, with 3,450 projectiles hitting the outside of the fort, 2,098 landing in its interior and just 1,757 missing Sumter altogether.[58] General Gillmore wrote:

> *The seven days service by the breaching batteries, ending August 23rd, left Fort Sumter in the condition of a mere infantry outpost, without the power to fire a gun heavier than a musket, alike incapable of annoying our approach on Battery Wagner, or of inflicting injury upon the fleet....A desultory fire was kept up to prevent repairs, and on the 30th of August, another severe cannonade was opened and continued for two days at the request of the admiral commanding, who contemplated entering the harbor on the 31st.*[59]

Destruction of Sumter was only a step toward the primary goal in the mind of Union general Quincy Gillmore. Charleston had long been a major target of the North for being at the center of secession and then for the firing on Fort Sumter in April 1861, an act considered by most to be the first shots of the war. Gillmore, who was masterfully conducting his army's operations on Morris Island, felt that, with Sumter now destroyed, he could take another step forward and compel the city of Charleston to surrender. The method chosen, however, was one that shocked the civilized world by its barbarous nature. He began shelling the city itself! An eight-inch Parrot rifle on Morris Island over five miles distant, dubbed "the Swamp Angel" by Union troops, opened fire on Charleston. The first shell was fired at 1:30 a.m. on August 22; fourteen others, most filled with incendiaries, quickly followed without warning. Any citizen in the lower end of the city, regardless of age, gender or color, was now a target. Gillmore sent Beauregard a demand that Fort Sumter and Morris Island be surrendered immediately. Beauregard returned a negative response with a scathing indictment reading in part, "Your firing a number of the most destructive missiles ever used in war into the midst of a city taken unawares and filled with sleeping women and children will give you a bad eminence in history."[60]

Gillmore agreed to cease his bombardment on the city for forty-eight hours to allow civilians to evacuate. On expiration of this time frame, the Swamp Angel resumed fire, mixing in incendiary shells with explosive ones before exploding on the thirty-sixth shot. Soon, however, other heavy cannon were set in place to bombard the city.[61] General Beauregard and others across the South issued vehement protests, but Gillmore, with no orders to the contrary from Washington, D.C., began a sustained bombardment of Charleston proper that lasted months. A Washington newspaper article, probably from early August, concerning bombardment of Charleston reflected the mood of the North against Charleston.

Fort Sumter's battle-damaged interior in a photograph from late 1863. *Library of Congress.*

*It is understood that Gen'l Gillmore has inquired of the government if he would be justified in bombarding Charleston to its utter destruction. The answer returned, it is said, was such as to give the country assurance of a heap of ashes where Charleston stands, if it does not surrender. A full supply of incendiary shells, to be hurled against Charleston, were sent to General Gillmore by the Arago, and by this time are probably being used against the doomed city.*[62]

General Pierre G.T. Beauregard in an 1861 sketch at Charleston. *Library of Congress*.

With all that was in progress, General Beauregard was deeply frustrated. The Yankees were able to fire on Fort Sumter and the city of Charleston at a range beyond any Confederate weaponry, rendering him helpless to reply in kind. He was also concerned about soon losing Fort Sumter and, on August 24, called for a panel of selected officers to rendezvous there to inspect the position and consider whether it could be held or should be abandoned. This group was composed of Colonel Alfred Rhett, Sumter's commander; Major Ormsby Blanding; Captain F.H. Harleston of the First South Carolina Artillery; Colonel J.F. Gilmer; Lieutenant Colonel D.B. Harris; and Lieutenant John Johnson from the Engineer Corps.[63]

The commission, having completed its inspection, met as a council and formally discussed the issues regarding Sumter. Each officer presented his thoughts in assessing the potential to hold the fort, what assets would be required to do so and what work would be required to provide a positive defensive posture for a body of troops occupying it. After much thoughtful and deliberate discussion, the commission's summary report was forwarded to Beauregard. Notably missing, however, was an opinion on whether the fort should be abandoned. However, Colonel Gilmer and Lieutenant Colonel Harris sent a joint opinion dated August 25 providing their shared view regarding this issue specifically. It read in part:

> [I]*n our opinion, it is not advisable to abandon the fort at this time. On the contrary, we think it should be held to the last extremity. How long it may be held is now only a matter of conjecture, but there are many elements of defense within the fort, in its present shattered position, which, if properly used, may enable a resolute garrison to hold it for many days. The question of its abandonment, whenever it may arise, we respectfully suggest should be determined by the commanding general, not left to the discretion of the commander of the fort.*[64]

General Beauregard was probably already inclined to hold the fort and likely would have done so of his own volition. One knowledgeable source close to Beauregard wrote in a postwar article that the decision was already made to hold Sumter: "One of the bravest officers in his command pronounced the work untenable. Beauregard then informed me that if necessary, he would go there and hold the fort with his staff; that on no condition would he consent to give it up to General Gillmore. It was after this that General (then Major) Stephen Elliott made his gallant defense of the ruins."[65]

The opinions of Gilmer and Harris confirmed Beauregard's decision to forego any thought of handing Sumter to the enemy, and the next day, he issued orders reading: "The opinion of Colonel Gilmer and Lieutenant-Colonel Harris, of the Engineers, is approved. Fort Sumter must be held to the last extremity, i.e., not surrendered until it becomes impossible to hold it any longer without an unnecessary sacrifice of human life. Evacuation of the fort must not be contemplated one instant without positive orders from these headquarters."[66]

The die was now cast. Sumter was to be held despite the expectations of soon losing Batteries Wagner and Gregg on Morris Island, which were now without artillery support from Sumter and subject to bombardment from land and sea. The fort's garrison would change from artillery to one of infantry, and the primary focus now shifted to selection of a commander and determining from where to draw the garrison. Beauregard apparently had spent time in anticipation of such a path and most likely built a short list of potential candidates to take command of the fort. Charleston had an abundance of capable infantry officers with distinguished service exemplified by personal acts of courage coupled with strong leadership. However, and for reasons never disclosed, he very quickly selected Stephen Elliott Jr., a major of artillery who had only recently arrived in Charleston, as the most tenable candidate in all of Charleston for the daunting task of commanding the fort. Beauregard, in a postwar article, simply stated without elaboration, "Major Elliott had been selected by me with care for that post of honor and danger."[67] Summoning Elliott to his headquarters, Beauregard went straight to the heart of the matter.

> *You are to be sent to a fort deprived of all offensive capacity, and having now but one gun—a 32-pounder—with which salute its flag, morning and evening. But that fort is Fort Sumter, the key to the entrance of this harbor. It must be held to the bitter end: not with artillery, as heretofore, but with infantry alone; and there can be no hope of reinforcements. Are you willing to take command on such terms? I desire that you shall take 24 hours to reflect, and that meanwhile you shall examine the fort, before making a final decision.*"[68]

Elliott must have been astounded at Beauregard's proposal. Certainly possessing at least a general awareness of the overall military situation around Charleston, he probably wondered why the offer to command such an important post in such perilous state had come to him. Whatever his

# Beaufort Legend, Charleston Hero

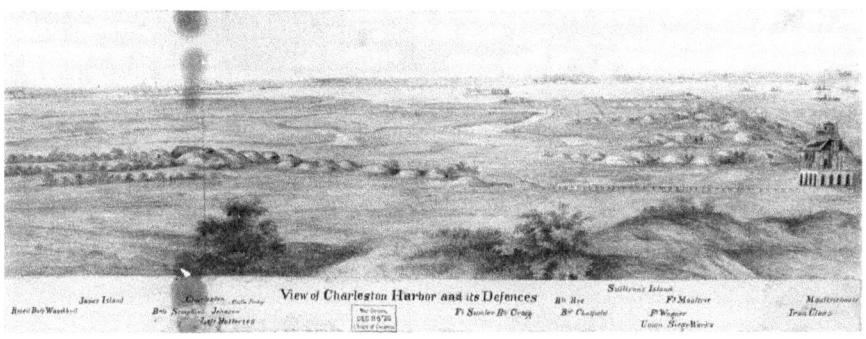

Wartime sketch of Charleston Harbor and its defenses. *Library of Congress*.

thoughts and apprehensions might have been that morning, he returned to Beauregard's headquarters later that same day and responded to the general's offer with, "I visited Sumter, and conferred with Colonel Rhett [Sumter's commanding officer]. Issue the order, General; I will obey it."[69] With that brief, concise and straightforward statement, Elliott accepted the daunting responsibility, knowing full well the inherent dangers and likely difficulties to be expected at Fort Sumter. Nothing in Beauregard's offer provided tangible enticements for acceptance. Why, then, would Elliott—or anyone else, for that matter—accept such an assignment? It was a call to step forward for duty at a particularly dangerous time at a post in imminent peril. Not only could reinforcements not be expected, there also was no avenue of retreat. If the enemy assaulted the fort in force, it would have to be stopped at the walls of the fort. Failing to do so was sure to result in the same situation faced by Colonel Travis, Jim Bowie, Davy Crockett and others at the Alamo in 1836: surrender or die. Tension from the situation enveloping Fort Sumter and Charleston, along with a sense of urgency in Beauregard's offer, were apparent. Elliott never explained why he answered Beauregard with a positive reply. One can surmise, however, that he saw the appointment in the same manner a soldier accepted appointment as regimental color-bearer knowing full well the imminent dangers of the position. It was a post of honor and recognition for one's proven heroism and good conduct in battle.[70]

On August 27, Beauregard sent a letter to General R.S. Ripley, commander of the First Military District, advising him of planned changes for Fort Sumter. In it, he explained that the garrison of Sumter was to be reduced to a company of artillery and two of infantry and maintained at a level of between two hundred and three hundred men. (This was amended on September 3 to an all-infantry garrison of two hundred muskets.) He added: "As the garrison will be so much reduced, it may be that Colonel Rhett will prefer to move the headquarters of his regiment....He has the option to do this or retain command of Fort Sumter. In the former event, Major Stephen Elliott will be assigned to the command of Fort Sumter."[71]

By offering him this option, Beauregard was displaying great courtesy toward Colonel Rhett, commanding officer of Fort Sumter and of the First South Carolina Artillery Regiment, a command that had garrisoned Fort Sumter since April 1861. Rhett had risen from lieutenant to his current rank through his efficiency and soldierly attributes. Highly energetic and solid in performance of his duties, Rhett performed magnificently in his various roles at Sumter. Beauregard showed his high esteem for Rhett just a few weeks after Rhett left Fort Sumter by sending the War Department a recommendation that Rhett be promoted in light of his distinguished and gallant service at Sumter. Nothing ever came of it.[72]

As for Stephen Elliott, he was about to embark on a mission far beyond any he had ever experienced or even heard of. There simply was no way for him to have foreseen the challenges, dangers and frustrations ahead of him. Elliott's August 28 letter to his wife clearly showed that he was prepared to take command of Sumter: "I am very proud of being selected for the position and am confident in my ability to do my duty with the assistance of my heavenly father."[73]

5

# POST OF HONOR: FORT SUMTER (SEPTEMBER–DECEMBER 1863)

Colonel Alfred Rhett held command of Sumter through September 4 before departing the next day to assume other duties pertaining to the defense of Charleston. In his final report as commanding officer of Fort Sumter, he wrote: "10 p.m., The Charleston Battalion arrived at the fort, under command of Major Stephen Elliott, and relieved Col. Alfred Rhett, commanding."[74] No doubt many were wondering if Major Stephen Elliott Jr. could perform as well as Rhett.

On September 5, a Saturday, Elliott started Sumter's next chapter by issuing General Order No. 1, which read, "In pursuance of special orders No. 298 par. III, I assume command at this fort."[75] The next day, in his first daily report to headquarters, he wrote, "I have the honor to make the following report; I assumed command of this post yesterday, pursuant to orders from department headquarters." He also gave the first indication that he was already actively reviewing the state of affairs at the fort by adding, "There are eighteen days rations for the present garrison, I would draw your attention to the fact there is no quartermaster at the post."[76]

This was the world Major Stephen Elliott entered on the evening of September 4, 1863. Nothing about the situation could be termed inspiring. Most other men would have been intimidated and overawed by the destruction seen at every turn. That, plus the anticipation of additional threats of continued bombardment from both land and sea together with possible direct assault by a small-boat attack were hardly encouraging. Fortunately, the interval from acceptance of Beauregard's offer and when he actually took command of the fort allowed Elliott time to mentally prepare for what lay ahead. Realizing the dangers and the seriousness of the situation encompassing Sumter and Charleston, he summoned his wits and courage and, driven by his personal sense of duty, arrived focused and prepared to carry out his assigned mission: defend Sumter!

His first day as commander of Fort Sumter was a hectic one filled with inspection, familiarization and organization. He was stepping into a position for which there was no precedent, one that would require him to be innovative and imaginative. Fortunately, not a shot was fired on the fort that day, allowing him uninterrupted opportunity to meet the officers and men of the Charleston Battalion and issue standing orders. One of these orders called for one-third of the garrison's three hundred infantry to be under arms on the parapet at night, with the balance in positions where they could quickly respond as needed if an enemy boat attack materialized. He formed grenade squads and Greek fire squads while ensuring that each company knew its assigned position.[77]

His impression of the Charleston Battalion was a good one, and he felt comfortable with the officers and the men who had previously performed admirably at Battery Wagner. A message sent asking that wood intended for bomb-proof shelters be sawed in the city as the fort lacked the facilities for doing so shows that Elliott was in deep conversation with the fort's engineers. The next day was also free of enemy fire on Sumter.[78]

Still, the winds of war surrounded him as Union guns pounded Battery Wagner. Confederate positions at various points nearby, in turn, fired their guns, trying to damage the enemy parallels advancing ever nearer to the position. From his vantage point at Sumter, Elliott could see firsthand the desperately intense situation at Wagner. That night, after fifty-eight days of battling against a determined foe supported with nearly unlimited resources, Batteries Wagner and Gregg were evacuated following a forty-two-hour bombardment from Union vessels and land artillery. Morris Island, just three quarters of a mile from Sumter, was now completely in enemy hands. The final goal of the Union army had been reached; now it was up to the navy to implement its part of the plan to take Charleston.

September 7 brought the war closer to Elliott's doorstep. At 10:00 a.m., a message was delivered to him under a flag of truce from Union admiral J.A. Dahlgren, commanding the U.S. Naval fleet off the coast of Charleston, demanding immediate surrender of Fort Sumter. Elliott telegraphed the contents to General Beauregard, advising him of the demand and adding, "I presume I shall refuse."[79] Beauregard's succinct reply to Elliott was a classic masterpiece conveying his resolve to hold the fort and rebuking the admiral at the same time. "Inform Admiral Dahlgren that he may have Fort Sumter when he can take and hold it; that such demands are puerile and unbecoming."[80] This defiant and inspirational reply became the battle cry for Fort Sumter. Beauregard had drawn the line in the sand, and there would be no turning back.[81] That night, Dahlgren sent several of his ironclads and armored vessels to bombard Fort Moultrie, comfortable in knowing Sumter could do nothing to harm them. While engaging Moultrie, the ships fired occasional shells into Sumter as if to taunt its garrison. Moultrie, however, showed its resolve and strength by inflicting severe damage on the Union ships.

September 8 was a relatively calm and quiet day at Sumter, allowing Elliott time to write a letter describing his present circumstances. Writing in a relaxed and confident manner, he said in part:

> *I am to hold the fort and repulse attack which I expect to do with ease. I allude of course to assault by barges....You have seen in the papers their demand for the fort and Gen'l Beauregard's reply....The engagement this morning was one of the most beautiful sites* [sic] *you can imagine. All the ironclads were within a mile of us and not firing on us at the time which improved the view considerably. They gave us almost thirty shots about half which struck....I feel quite contented...as I have tried to do everything I could think of to beat the scamps off and as far as the shelling it is not what it was in an open field....The fort was taken today by "Cook, artist."*[82]

The engagement with Fort Moultrie was evidently intended to be a "softening up" measure, because possession of Fort Sumter remained paramount in the minds of both General Gillmore and Admiral Dahlgren. Each, thinking Sumter was held only by a corporal's guard but without informing the other, planned a boat assault with a heavy force against Sumter for the early-morning hours of September 9. Only in the afternoon the day before did the two officers learn of each other's plans. Offers to cooperate were respectfully declined. Capture of Sumter would increase the prestige of the branch of service seizing it. Accordingly, Sumter was targeted by one group of assault boats manned by the army and another comprising sailors and marines.

About 1:00 a.m. on September 9, Major Stephen Elliott was on the wall of the fort with his chief engineering officer, Captain John T. Champneys. They were watching a single Yankee monitor suspiciously moving into a position threatening Sumter when his attention was diverted to the approach of two columns of small boats. These were the naval contingent, at least four hundred strong. Quickly alerting and ordering the garrison to their pre-planned stations, Elliott watched as eighty men with muskets and twenty-four others armed with grenades and fireballs manned the wall. The remaining garrison troops took positions in different sectors of the fort, each ready to support those on the wall if needed. Elliott passed the word not to open fire until a landing was made and waited with anticipation as the boats came nearer and nearer. When the leading boats arrived and began unloading, a horrific fire opened on them from above. It was immediately apparent to the surprised Yankees that they were in trouble. Musketry, grenades and even thrown stone rubble rained down on them. Two nearby fougasse sites were ignited, adding to the confusion. Rockets from Sumter were fired, alerting other Confederate commands that an attack was taking place. Despite the chaos in the early moments and the realization that they were facing far more than a corporal's guard, the Yankees who had landed bravely attempted to scale the walls but got nowhere. In desperation, their resolve to continue the assault turned to finding refuge in the fort's rubble after cannon fire from Fort Moultrie and Fort Johnson, as well as the guns of the Confederate gunboat *Chicora*, opened on them with grape and canister. The boats that had not landed turned away from the fort and began hastily rowing toward their starting point, greatly inspired by the guns of the *Chicora* now turned on them. Those left behind, realizing the assault could not be continued and escape was virtually impossible, surrendered.

One Union officer in the attack accurately described the scene in his report with a concise description of the action. "As soon as the boats were discovered, they were met with a fire of musketry, hand-grenades, lighted shells, and grape and canister; and simultaneously, at a signal from the fort, all the enemies batteries surrounding us, with one of their gunboat rams, opened fire....All who landed were either killed or taken prisoners, and serious casualties occurred in the boats near the fort."[83] Another Union officer wrote, "Five thousand men could not have captured the fort that night."[84]

Herded into the fort, they were quickly disarmed and made prisoners of war. One of the prisoners was a senior naval officer of the expedition, Lieutenant Commander E.P. Williams, who later reported that the prisoners "were courteously treated by Major Elliott....The wounded were well treated by the enemy."[85] It was a complete victory for Major Elliott and his men and a humiliating defeat for Admiral Dahlgren, who had confidently expected to see the flag of the United States atop Sumter at daybreak that morning.

Elliott quickly advised Beauregard of the failed attempt to capture Sumter with the basic details and followed with a formal and highly detailed report on September 12. In summary, the assaulting force had numbered at least 400 men (Dahlgren gave figures of 400 men and 500 men at different times), but captured documentation indicated as many as 870 sailors and marines were involved. Half a dozen Yankees were killed, 15 were wounded and 106 others were captured uninjured in the twenty-minute fight. It is likely that others were killed by the guns of the *Chicora*, as several empty and overturned boats were found adrift the next day. Additionally, five of the enemy's barges were captured along with five stands of colors and a number of small arms. Elliott wrote, "The action was brief and decisive, as they found us prepared, and were themselves surprised at meeting more than a nominal resistance."[86] He was liberal with praise for the officers and men who had performed so well. Among the materials captured was a "worn and torn" U.S. garrison flag that some prisoners claimed was the same one lowered at Sumter by Major Robert Anderson in April 1861 when he surrendered the fort to Confederate forces. The flag reportedly had been sent to add even more delight and pleasure for the North in the recapture of Sumter. Though there were doubts about its authenticity, it remained a war prize.[87]

General Gillmore's assault force, comprising two regiments, was still ashore awaiting high tide when Dahlgren's men landed at the fort, causing the army's planned assault to be canceled. Gillmore and Dahlgren each suffered with the great disappointment of having such a coveted target, thought to be extremely vulnerable, escape their clutches.

Beauregard telegraphed the War Department in Richmond that morning advising of the engagement and its outcome. J.A. Seddon, the secretary of war, responded that same day acknowledging the battle and, at the same time, the perils Charleston had faced the past couple of days: "Your telegrams, informing of the repulse of the iron-clads, and of the brilliant affair at Sumter, have been received with the liveliest satisfaction. We watch with intense anxiety the progress of your noble struggle....The brave defenders of Charleston are honored and relied on throughout the Confederacy."[88] Beauregard also sent a message to Elliott complimenting him and his garrison for their brilliant success. Additionally, he addressed the subject of prisoners at Sumter: "[Beauregard] will endeavor to have the prisoners removed in the course of the day or tonight. Should the enemy meanwhile bombard Sumter, and you have not enough cover for your command, you will expose the prisoners, instead of your troops, to the enemy's fire."[89] Bodies of the marines and sailors killed in the assault were sent under a flag of truce to the Union fleet late that afternoon.[90] Fortunately, Sumter was not subjected to shelling again until September 28.

## Confederate General Stephen Elliott

STEPHEN ELLIOTT HAD REASON to be excited and proud. His first test as commander of Sumter had proved his mettle and removed any doubts that he, or others, might have had about his ability. His defensive plan, contrived the very first day in command, proved to be decisive and very much appropriate. Beauregard, too, was elated. For a change, he could report good news from Charleston. Further, his choice of commanding officer at Sumter, though an officer of artillery, had shown himself totally worthy and capable of the post. Both Elliott and Beauregard must have appreciated that General Ripley had heeded instructions and sent a high-quality command in the form of the Charleston Battalion to Sumter. They were the right troops at the right place at the right time.

Elliott's name was properly mentioned in newspaper reports of the engagement, and to many, he was immediately seen as a hero. One Charleston newspaper, the *Mercury*, reported, "We have received, from a Lady, a beautiful silk tobacco pouch for Major Stephen Elliott, Jr., which we have forwarded as requested."[91]

Beauregard sent another telegram to Richmond on September 9. In it, he pleaded for recognition for Elliott in the form of immediate promotion: "I beg to recommend Maj. Stephen Elliott commanding Sumter for promotion. He is brave, zealous & efficient. He has under his command a battalion commanded by a Major."[92] Such a promotion would prevent any likelihood of conflict with an officer of equal rank while, at the same time, provide recognition for Elliott's brilliant work in defending Sumter against the assault. Unfortunately, because of technicalities, this recommendation would languish in Richmond in a manner similar to his promotion to major. Normally, a lieutenant colonel of artillery commanded at least a battalion of artillery consisting of multiple batteries. Elliott's posting technically had no relationship at all to artillery, and under the restraints of army regulations, such a promotion was not something the War Department could easily approve despite the merit warranting it.

Painting of Stephen Elliott Jr. as a major at Fort Sumter by James Reeve Stuart. *By the permission of the Beaufort History Museum, Beaufort S.C.*

It was apparent to all that any Union attack on Sumter would be a perilous one regardless of its nature. Though it possessed no offensive firepower, the fort was well covered by interlocking fire from other positions in the harbor and manned by sufficient troops under a highly competent and vigilant commander. General Gillmore and Admiral Dahlgren were now stymied as to their next move. Gillmore saw the role assigned him and his land forces in the quest to take Sumter and Charleston as being completed when Morris Island was secured. Dahlgren realized that the onus now was completely on him. Gillmore advised Dahlgren that he could still provide artillery support by moving guns forward to Battery Wagner and, even closer to Sumter, to Cummings Point. However, it was clearly understood by all that the next move to take Sumter or Charleston belonged to Dahlgren and the navy. For the next nineteen days, Fort Sumter was free from any shelling as Gillmore's men were occupied with the laborious task of relocating their heavy guns and reestablishing the batteries in forward positions.

While maintaining a vigilant awareness for further threats, Major Elliott was able to turn his attention to other needs of the fort, calling on his skills as an administrator while becoming acclimated to the world of construction engineering. A number of demands requiring his attention and concern were quickly apparent. First, foremost and always, defense of Fort Sumter remained the paramount issue, followed closely by the livability for the garrison and problems with logistics and supply. Each of these was a pressing matter requiring daily involvement and close attention. Another key point of concern, restoring Fort Sumter into a credible and contributing military post, was a long-range goal that few expected to be reached. Any and all decisions within the fort were his, and a misstep along the way could have adverse results. His post was certainly that of an independent command requiring a clear-thinking commander possessing a unique mixture of positive attributes, including foresight, clear judgment and the ability to encourage and maintain high morale in the tight confines of the fort.

Elliott certainly had his work cut out for him in trying to juggle this array of matters, for he had little in the way of personal staff to assist him. The only other permanent military member of the fort's complement was an engineer, Captain John T. Champneys, assigned by the Engineer Department in Charleston. Like Elliott, he was highly capable, motivated and energetic. A native Charlestonian with a strong background in ordnance, Champneys had served with distinction at Battery Wagner as well as at Sumter under Colonel Rhett and volunteered to remain at the fort when Rhett was relieved. The two men were a perfect tandem for meeting the demands facing them, and Elliott gave Champneys worthy commendation for his actions during the small-boat assault. In addition, a post surgeon, an adjutant, a quartermaster, Signal Corps members and a commissary officer were available but rotated on a regular basis. The civilian telegrapher stayed throughout Elliott's service at Sumter. Champneys had an engineering party with junior officers and civilians who worked very well together. Elliott seems to have handled most communications from the fort himself rather than going through an adjutant. Nearly all entries in his Order and Letters Books are in his own hand. Much depended on him, and at times, the loneliness of such a command likely rested on his shoulders like a huge weight. Fortunately, he had ready access to Beauregard and did not hesitate to utilize it. To his credit, Beauregard realized full well the difficulties Elliott faced and provided full support in addressing or, whenever possible, easing some of the burdens and problems brought to his attention. There are definite signs of mutual trust and respect in the interaction of these two men in the following months.

Having little staff, Elliott depended on the officers of the infantry contingent assigned to the fort to carry out certain functions. The senior officer among them was designated to take command of the fort in case of emergency. Elliott closely scrutinized these officers and spent substantial time and energy in ensuring that each fully understood the role he was expected to carry out in the event of enemy attack. He realized that defending a fort was far different than the customary field duty that infantry was trained for and experienced. He probably anticipated that some of the men were uncomfortable in being assigned to such a battered ruin on an isolated island. The fort offered no avenue of retreat and was subject to horrific bombardment, but Elliott depended on the officers to keep these concerns from affecting the performance expected of them. With the infantry commands being relieved and replaced on a regular basis, this orientation was a time-consuming and repetitive, but crucial, process. In his eight-month post as commander of Sumter, not a single company of infantry was assigned there more than once.

Quarters at Sumter were crude and less than comfortable. There was little interior space in the lower casemates to accommodate or provide shelter from shelling for those assigned to the post or to hold large quantities of supplies. Sumter was entirely dependent on regular delivery of supplies such as rations, as well as other necessities like candles, oil for lanterns, medicines and, above all else, water. The fort's cistern system had been destroyed during the recent bombardment, and availability of water was an immediate and paramount concern. Regular and uninterrupted arrival of supply steamers was an absolute necessity to sustain those in the fort. These same vessels carried away the fort's wounded and sick, as well as the dead, on their return trip to Charleston.

CONFEDERATE ENGINEERS AT SUMTER were active, energetic and efficient in their work aimed toward completion of three major projects. Headed by Captain Champneys, excavation was begun to recover the fort's guns from the rubble and return them to Charleston for use elsewhere. At the same time, plans were being developed to enlarge and enhance areas of the fort for protective shelter and storage. Finally, intertwined with the other goals and bearing perhaps the most important need at the moment was the matter of the fort's security. Strengthening weak spots to thwart assaults by small boats was an ongoing priority for months to come.

The lack of Union bombardment from September 9 to 28 was a gift to Sumter's engineers. Work parties carried a multitude of chores and supervised activities taking place on a round-the-clock basis. Utilizing small parties of Negro laborers supplemented by details from the fort's garrison, rubble was removed from some of the bottom tier casemates. Sandbags delivered by supply steamers at night were filled and placed in strategic locations to strengthen walls, giving added protection against shellfire and splintering. Guns recovered were loaded onto the steamers as quickly as possible. Quarters and shelter for the garrison, engineers and others assigned to the fort were crude and spartan but became much more serviceable over time.

Captain Champneys was the key man in all of these endeavors. His work, plans and suggestions were regularly monitored by senior officers of the Engineer Corps in Charleston, and by all accounts they provided him all possible support. Major Elliott, as fort commander, certainly spent a great deal of time with Champneys. He was privy to the daily plans and status reports and provided assistance whenever possible, including utilizing garrison troops at times to provide additional labor. Elliott depended on Champneys's engineering skills, foresight and ability to juggle his work with limited resources in such a vulnerable environment.

Elliott's daily routine in these quiet days generally consisted of keeping abreast of the progress of the engineers; handling communications among the fort, Charleston and its outposts; and receiving high-level visitors such as General Beauregard, members of his staff and other senior officers—all the while ensuring that all matters concerning the fort's activities and security ran smoothly. Elliott was also tasked with observing and reporting shipping activity off Charleston Harbor. His report of September 22, similar to many others he submitted, reads: "There are inside the bar this morning the Ironsides, four monitors, one sloop of war, four gunboats, three mortar boats, and twenty-nine other vessels. Seven vessels off the bar, including a French and an English sloop of war. Several vessels arrived today from both the north and south; and though some of them were loaded, none brought troops."[93]

Further, he took it on himself to issue regular reports on enemy activities on Morris Island, with the nearest point just thirteen hundred yards away. This must have been an agonizing period for him, as he could plainly see his foe working on modifying Batteries Wagner and Gregg to their liking. On September 13, he reported, "The enemy still continue silent, but are working industriously at Battery Wagner, altering its shape and mounting guns."[94] Three days later, he advised Beauregard, "The enemy are still working on Battery Gregg and exposing themselves with impunity."[95] The next day, he reported, "Long trains of wagons…coming down the beach on Morris Island, and discharging their contents at Battery Gregg."[96] On September 19, his report read, "The enemy continues to work industriously by strengthening old batteries and erecting new ones on Morris Island, placing guns in position at Wagner."[97] These concise and factual daily reports convey no hint of fear, anxiety or foreboding. What emotions or apprehensions he had remained veiled.

Elliott certainly anticipated that Fort Sumter would soon be targeted again from the very positions he was observing, and he was totally helpless to prevent it. Further still, he had no way to respond. Fort Sumter was a static post without benefit of being able to advance, maneuver or retreat; as such, it was simply a large, motionless target for an enemy with seemingly unlimited resources and the heaviest guns in the world. Yet, it was his duty to defend and hold it regardless of what happened unless otherwise instructed by General Beauregard.

However, the Yankees were not the only ones busy. The Charleston Battalion was relieved in full on September 19 by 250 men of Elliott's old regiment, the Eleventh South Carolina Volunteer Infantry.[98] This change necessitated Elliott taking substantial time to familiarize the men with the fort, its conditions and his expectations. He would certainly have taken pains to impress upon their officers what their roles consisted of and to ensure that the senior captain was fully aware of any contingency plans should an emergency arise and Elliott be unavailable.

On September 21, Captain Champneys's engineering work provided Elliott an almost unimaginable opportunity to announce good news. In a message to Beauregard's headquarters, Elliott wrote: "I have the honor to report that I consider this work still capable of offensive operations. The arches of four of the lower casemates on the north-eastern front face are uninjured...and to a great extent protected above and in the rear."[99] This positive news meant that guns could be placed to cover the seaward approach to Sumter. The very next day, Major General J.F. Gilmer, Beauregard's senior subordinate, accompanied by his chief engineer, visited Sumter to examine the possibility Elliott presented. After a lengthy inspection, they reached the same conclusion.[100] Gilmer's report confirmed that three heavy guns could be reasonably protected if placed in position as Elliott proposed. Work would soon begin to bring this about. The fort had evacuated all but eleven cannon at this point, and now it appeared that three of those would be mounted and prepared to contest any movement by the Union navy attempting to enter the harbor.

The next day, there was great jubilation in Charleston and across the South on receiving news of the tremendous Confederate victory at Chickamauga, Georgia. Beauregard ordered a National Salute be fired in celebration of this crucial victory.[101] While it didn't erase the pains of Gettysburg and Vicksburg, this news raised the spirits of Southerners everywhere. Also on September 23, Beauregard issued an inquiry to General Ripley asking if Fort Sumter was amply provided with water. He also directed that Sumter be furnished with disinfectant and that, instead of exchanging full battalions en masse at Sumter, that one company of the garrison be exchanged each week.[102] Elliott had previously noted water shortages at Sumter and on September 16 placed a daily ration of just one gallon a day per man for all purposes. This limit lasted until October 18, when the ration was increased to one and one-half gallons.[103]

Not all was good at Sumter, though. Apparently without going into details, Elliott asked that the senior captain of his garrison and his entire Eleventh South Carolina Infantry company be removed and replaced. Elliott stated that the captain was "incompetent to command the fort" in an emergency. On the night of September 27–28, a company from the Twenty-Fifth South Carolina Infantry arrived with a senior captain, and the other company departed. The new captain, now designated the senior line officer of the garrison, was believed by his superiors to be suitable for Elliott's needs.[104] This was a drastic move, and the fact that it was handled so quickly and efficiently reflects the complete and total attention Beauregard's headquarters paid to Elliott and affairs at Sumter.

That same night, the water-boat failed to deliver that precious commodity to Sumter. Major Elliott's anger clearly showed in his dispatch advising Beauregard of the matter: "Commander of water-boat is an arrant coward, and if the boat is not seized and placed under military control, we will not get our full supply of water."[105] With about four hundred men at Sumter, including the garrison troops, engineers and their working parties, plus the other assorted postings, water was an absolute necessity, and failure to deliver it was a severe breach of a vital responsibility. For this to happen under a period of rationing was simply unacceptable and Elliott's fury was fully justified.

September 28, already a bad day, turned even worse at 1:45 that afternoon. Enemy guns opened on Sumter for the first time in nearly three weeks. Union batteries from Morris Island and over two miles away from the fort fired exactly 100 shots, of which 48 hit. Shelling of Sumter continued for another five days, causing little damage; just two men, one a Negro workman, were wounded. A total of 560 shots were fired at Sumter over the six days, with 324 hitting.[106] This period, termed a "minor bombardment," served notice that Sumter had not been forgotten and could be targeted at any time. In the preceding weeks, Union artillery had been very active, but against other Confederate positions in the harbor area. In the weeks following this "minor bombardment," the enemy resumed firing on other targets and left Sumter alone until October 26.

1863 photograph of one-hundred-pound Union Parrott rifles on Morris Island used against Fort Sumter and other Confederate positions in Charleston's harbor. *Library of Congress*.

This six-day barrage had little effect on the work at Sumter. On October 1, engineers were able to report that the last of the available lead and copper there was removed from the post. By then, they had also removed sufficient debris and strengthened enough walls and overheads to allow additional quarters for another one hundred men.[107] Still, the bombardment was sufficient in size and duration to remind Elliott and those with him of their vulnerability. It also served as a motive to hasten work on the fort. On October 5, Elliott suggested that additional sandbags, as many as two thousand, be provided to him each night to secure breached walls.[108]

THE NEXT THREE WEEKS at Sumter were free from enemy shelling, and Elliott could watch enemy guns on Morris Island fire on other Confederate positions around Charleston and, in turn, receive counter-battery fire from them. The city of Charleston remained under heavy bombardment of Union guns. The Yankees continued their work on Batteries Wagner and Gregg and, despite shelling by guns from Fort Moultrie, made daily progress. Elliott made numerous reports on the effects of the Confederate shots, which, while often causing casualties and damage, caused only temporary stoppages of Union activities. Still, any delay to the enemy brought more time to strengthen Sumter.

Major Elliott was always concerned and anxious for the welfare of those he commanded and, on October 10, displayed his awareness of the hardships for the troops in the fort. That day, he sent a request to Beauregard advising that the rations provided his garrison were inadequate. "[They] are exposed to the night air without intermission…frequently employed in labor…and entirely cutoff from the fortuitous supplies offered by sutlers at more accessible points.…I request that an addition of a half ration…a meal be added."[109]

Further, on the fifteenth, he sent a request that the men and officers of Companies H and I of the Eleventh South Carolina be granted five days' furlough when relieved from Sumter. "It will be a grateful act of kindness and even justice to men who have stood up to severe duty without a complaint." Elliott held these men in high regard, for they had been at Sumter since September 15, endured the six-day barrage, labored on the fort while on strict water rationing and, as he noted, had only a few "casually sick" in that period. This was the only way he had to provide due recognition of their service.[110] They were relieved on the night of September 18–19 by a contingent from the Twelfth Georgia Battalion Light Artillery serving as infantry. Again, Major Elliott had to devote substantial time explaining conditions of the fort to the new garrison, organizing it to fit the needs and ensuring that the officers and enlisted men alike knew and understood their assigned roles in event of an emergency.

Work continued at a feverish pace in Sumter. Shipments of coal and iron, retrieved from the rubble, were shipped from the fort on three consecutive nights.[111] Sandbags and cotton bales were placed, rubble was removed from the casemates and work on improvements of shelter and defenses continued. Sumter was indeed in full recovery mode, bringing with it an optimistic mood. The crowning moment occurred on October 14 with the mounting of three heavy guns facing Charleston's channel entrance. This monumental achievement was a credit to Captain Champneys, who headed the engineering efforts, and to Stephen Elliott, who pushed hard to bring it about. Termed the "Three-Gun Battery," it represented a new dimension of the fort still rising from the ruins.[112]

Adding to the fort's defenses, Elliott and his engineers devised a series of booms composed of heavy logs anchored off the weak spots of the fort with wire entanglements on the shore to obstruct boat landings. Additionally, a series of fraises—sharpened wooden spikes commonly used on battlefield entrenchments—was placed on the slopes above the wire. Set in frames, these impediments would substantially retard any assaulting troops trying to reach the upper part of the fort. Sumter's engineers placed and retrieved each of these defensive obstacles each night. Mountain howitzers requested by Elliott, placed in key positions nightly and withdrawn before daybreak,

Sketch of the Three-Gun Battery mounted in October 1863. *Library of Congress.*

Sketch of the entrance to the Three-Gun Battery established in October 1863. *Library of Congress.*

added to Sumter's ability to withstand and repel any boat attacks. The Yankees never learned of their presence.[113]

Elliott ensured that tight vigilance was maintained during the day, looking for any hint of another boat assault that might be forming. At night, sentries often saw him walking the ramparts ensuring their watchfulness. Union commanders regularly sent small-boat patrols to test the fort's alertness; these, at times, caused the entire garrison to be called out.[114] On the night of October 21, sentries at Fort Johnson noticed several enemy barges and opened on them with grapeshot, which drove them away. Presumably, the enemy was either trying to cut Sumter's telegraph cable or place a line on it but fled before either could be accomplished.[115]

OCTOBER 26 WAS NOT a good day at Sumter. First, Major Elliott issued an edict to the garrison that the post whiskey rations would be drawn only by the company commanders, who would ensure that the rations would be consumed immediately upon being distributed to their men. Elliott further stated, "If any more troubles occur all issues will be stopped and no more liquor will be allowed to reach the post."[116] The cause for this order is not stated, but Elliott could not allow anything having a negative effect on defense of Sumter to continue. In this instance, he obviously intended that the warning would have the desired effect without depriving the troops of this little luxury.

The other bad thing, and far more important, was that the Yankees commenced bombardment of Fort Sumter again. With the navy continuously delaying any attempt to take Charleston as planned, General Gillmore ordered the bombardment to destroy the Three-Gun Battery he had learned was in place. His information, however, was not completely correct. The battery was in the northeastern part of the fort; Gillmore's intelligence sources led him to believe it was in the southeastern part. Accordingly, the direct fire of his multitude of guns was incorrectly aligned for the purpose Gillmore claimed.[117]

At 12:30 p.m., Gillmore's guns opened fire on Forts Sumter, Johnson and Moultrie. Firing in a slow and deliberate manner at Sumter, the Yankee artillery fired 165 shots, none of which missed. During the shelling, a Yankee wood-hulled gunboat and a monitor closed on Fort Sumter long enough to hurl 32 heavy shells but scored only 9 hits before retiring.[118] Firing on October 27 began at 7:00 a.m., with enemy troops lining the dunes and beaches of Morris Island to witness the firing on Sumter. Elliott had several sharpshooters armed with long-range Whitworth rifles in the fort. To their credit, they focused their firing on enemy gunners at Battery Gregg. The barrage continued with additional fire from Battery Wagner, another nearby battery and, at one point, from enemy monitors. A total of 766 shots were fired on Sumter, with 648 of them striking.[119]

October 28 brought more of the same. Mortar fire and heavy Parrott rifles continued to rain fire on Sumter from near-point-blank range. Of the 798 shells fired, 703 hit the fort. Work inside was drastically reduced by now. The mortars at Cummings Point, huge thirteen-inch monster guns weighing as much as five thousand pounds each, fired projectiles weighing two hundred pounds into Sumter. The Parrott rifles threw shells weighing two hundred and three hundred pounds, along with some thirty-pounders, into the walls and structures of the fort.

On October 29, Major Elliott had additional worries added to his shoulders, leading him to send a message to Beauregard advising that not a single captain of the Twelfth Georgia Battalion was present and expressed fears that their absence might adversely affect their men at the fort if an

1863 photograph of eight-inch Union Parrott rifles on Morris Island used against Fort Sumter and other Confederate installations in Charleston's harbor. *Library of Congress.*

emergency arose. Most of the captains were reported as being absent on sick certificates, but he had information they were fit for duty. Beauregard's headquarters began an immediate search for them for the purpose of returning them to the fort.[120] That same day, a total of 1,030 shells from the Morris Island batteries and monitors were fired at Sumter, scoring 870 hits on the fort's walls or inside them. The next day brought another heavy pounding, with 1,019 shells fired at the fort, of which 943 struck. The shelling slacked off considerably each night, allowing supply ships to reach Sumter with their precious cargo.

October 31, the sixth day of bombardment, began in a grim manner. A squad of thirteen men, part of a ready reaction force should a boat assault take place, was sleeping with arms and accoutrements in what was believed to be a safe place. At 3:00 a.m., a Union shell squarely hit a steel girder supporting the ceiling and knocked it away. The ceiling, with tons of rubble above it, fell on the men, killing them all. Most were Charleston citizens from Company A, the Washington Light Infantry, Twenty-Fifth South Carolina Infantry, who had arrived at the fort in late September, replacing the banished company of the Eleventh South Carolina. Their loss was felt throughout the garrison, and the manner in which they died would certainly have increased the sense of vulnerability of those at Sumter. Two others were killed and four were wounded that day by enemy fire, bringing the

Wartime photograph of Union mortars on Morris Island used against Fort Sumter. *Library of Congress.*

six-day bombardment casualty total to sixteen dead and fifteen wounded.[121] The enemy fired 1,005 shells at the fort on the thirty-first, achieving 802 hits and bringing the total shots fired at Sumter the last six days of the month to 4,825, of which just 675 missed their target.[122]

The *Charleston Mercury*, a prominent newspaper, mentioned the ongoing bombardment on October 31. The article read in part:

> *The enemy still continues to concentrate his fire upon Sumter. On Thursday night two hundred and sixty shots were directed at the fort—a hundred and eighty of which struck their target. Friday witnessed one of the most vigorous bombardments which has taken place since the beginning of the siege....* [It] *was sufficient to test severely the strength of the works and the fortitude of the garrison commanded by Major Stephen Elliott, Jr., whose steadiness, conduct and capacity have often been tried, and never found wanting.*[123]

The day included, of all things, a semimonthly inspection of Sumter that found that, despite the circumstances, the fort's police and sanitary measures were being carried on as effectively as possible. Other things caught Major Elliott's eyes, though. The additional damage to the walls and interior of the fort caused much difficulty in reaching the ramparts, a situation that would be serious if attacked by boats. Elliott's clear thinking led him to issue a request for a number of ladders, fifteen feet in length, on which the garrison could mount the parapets in a quicker and less difficult manner.[124]

However badly the day began, it ended on a bright note of valor and defiance that inspired all within Fort Sumter. The fort's garrison flag was twice shot away that day and replaced by three members of the Twelfth Georgia Battalion. If Stephen Elliott had doubts about their captains, their men showed him by these actions that he should have none toward them. Finally, the garrison flag was so badly torn from shot and shell that the same men who had replaced it earlier, including the battalion color-bearer, planted the battle flag of the Twelfth Georgia Battalion on the ramparts. When it, too, was cut down, the same three men recovered it, determined that a battle flag was going to be kept flying. Two of them, one having to stand on the shoulders of another, set it in place again. Each of these acts of replacing the flag was in full view of the enemy, and the men were in mortal danger each time. These heroic deeds were not the last displayed by the battalion that day. In the late afternoon, with shelling still occurring, the band of the Twelfth Georgia marched into an opening along the fort wall facing Morris Island and struck up the song "Bonnie Blue Flag," at which time the firing on Sumter ceased. Soon, a Yankee band appeared on the beach and played "The Star-Spangled Banner." One of the men at Sumter later wrote, "The cheers of the sailors on the monitors and from the Federal garrisons on Morris Island were definitely heard at Fort Sumter, despite the roar of artillery."[125] The valiant trio who kept a flag flying atop Sumter that day was cited by name in Elliott's reports that evening.[126] After a short lull, the bombardment picked up again, but it was apparent to all in this brief event that the men in Sumter were nowhere close to being whipped or demoralized. Stephen Elliott certainly had reason to be confident in his garrison, and the Yankees had to wonder what kind of men could withstand such punishment and still retain such spirit.

November 1, 1863, was the 113th day of the siege of Charleston, and the new month started the same way October ended, with a continuation of the bombardment. General Beauregard's message to Richmond that day conveyed his attitude toward Sumter: "Bombardment of Sumter has continued steadily since yesterday....Damage considerable, but not vital. Ruins of fort will be defended to last extremity."[127]

Stephen Elliott probably was quite concerned, as his entire garrison was relieved that night and replaced by a mixture of companies from a variety of regiments.[128] Organizing and acclimating this new garrison to Sumter in the midst of Yankee shelling was not an easy task but one that certainly had to be performed without delay, and presumably, Elliott met this untimely challenge efficiently and patiently. Still, he likely sent a reminder that previous orders called for the relief of the garrison by one third weekly, for, just two days later, Beauregard issued another order specifically instructing that the garrison be relieved in one-hundred-man detachments every fourth or fifth night.[129]

The very next night, one of the replacements almost made a grievous mistake while on sentry duty. A boat with four Yankee scouts quietly approached the fort and was detected only when it landed and two men began moving toward the wall. The sentry, thinking it was a friendly picket boat, challenged the pair but did not give an alarm. After a brief period of conversation with them, he realized they were Yankees and took appropriate action. With the garrison roused, the scouts returned to the boat and hastily pulled away amid a hail of musketry, which wounded one of them.[130]

The complete replacement of his garrison could not have come at a worse time for Stephen Elliott. Confederate president Jefferson Davis arrived in Charleston on November 1 and began a tour of several areas in and around the city. Further, several messages advising of the possibility of a small-boat attack on Sumter and elsewhere in the harbor were received and weighed on Elliott's mind.[131] Davis, Beauregard and the governor of South Carolina, along with other high dignitaries, made their way to several locations for inspection tours around Charleston. One stop was near Fort Moultrie, and from there they could clearly see the shambles of Fort Sumter across the narrow harbor channel and witnessed some of the ongoing bombardment of the fort from the guns of monitors and Union batteries on Morris Island.[132] Undoubtedly, Elliott's name was mentioned frequently in a prominent and complimentary manner during the stop.

On November 6, with President Davis having departed Charleston and destined for Wilmington, General Beauregard sent a message to Davis. "I visited Sumter last night. It is all right at the present. Major Elliott and garrison are in fine spirits....Commanding officer of that post should have more rank."[133]

Beauregard's September 9 recommendation for Elliott's promotion was still in limbo in Richmond, and by appealing directly to President Davis, Beauregard was apparently hoping Davis would use his authority to bring the promotion to fruition, especially after having seen what Fort Sumter was enduring with his own eyes.

The bombardment of Sumter continued daily. Garrison exchanges fell into the prescribed pattern of 100 men every few days, and Union small boats continued showing up around the fort, testing its vigilance. On the night of November 17, alarm was sounded four different times due to nearby presence of enemy boats. The escalation in activity concerned Elliott, and vigilance at the fort was increased. Early in the morning of November 20, just a day after one-third of the garrison was relieved by a new contingent, Elliott realized the conditions were ripe for a boat assault. There was no moon, and weather conditions were quite mild. At 2:30 a.m., he called for the garrison to be awakened and placed into their assigned

Fort Sumter's shattered interior in late 1863. *Library of Congress.*

positions within the fort. Expecting the men to quickly file out under arms to their assigned areas, he received disturbing news that every commanding officer fears: some soldiers refused to obey their orders. A number of men from two different commands that had been at the fort since November 10 refused to mount the parapet despite encouragement and pleas by others of their command. Before the situation could be resolved, several enemy barges loaded with troops were sighted rapidly approaching the fort and, in a short while, opened on the fort with musketry from under three hundred yards. Despite orders not to shoot unless told to do so, many soldiers began returning fire and, shortly afterward, the enemy boats departed.[134] A Union report stated that the affair was simply a reconnaissance in force consisting of 250 men intended to test the fort's vigilance and draw its fire so an estimate of its strength could be made. The Union commander wrote: "No assault was to be made unless it was evident that it could be taken easily.... The garrison appears to have been on the watch."[135] A report to General Gillmore stated: "The reconnaissance was as ordered. The boats were met with a heavy fire...estimate 200 muskets. We had 2 men wounded."[136] Elliott must have been beside himself and terribly disappointed at the lack of discipline displayed that night, for he could certainly have duplicated the victory of September 9.

When the threat was over, Elliott showed true leadership. In his report of the action that morning, he gave a clear, concise account of what had transpired, including the refusal of troops to man their posts. The only name he mentioned was that of a lieutenant who had displayed courage and set an example for others to follow. He added, "I have sent a dispatch to General Taliaferro, asking him to relieve two lieutenants who did not behave well. I have not evidence enough to convict them, but do not want them here any longer. I have taken measures which I trust may insure [sic] better conduct in the future."[137] Both officers were removed from the fort the next evening and replaced with other lieutenants from the same regiments. What measures Elliott took are not found, but it is striking that he expelled the two lieutenants but none of the enlisted men who had refused to take their positions. However, this is the only instance of such misconduct Elliott experienced while in command of Fort Sumter.

A week later, another act of heroism involving the fort's battle flag occurred. A private, seeing the flag shot away, disregarded his own safety by walking in full view of the enemy to retrieve the fallen banner. On gathering it, he attempted to raise it again, but the staff was too short. Obtaining an additional piece of wood, and with assistance from three other enlisted men inspired by the private's actions, the pieces were spliced together. But, as they were about to set the staff in place, a Yankee shell hit it and took it from their hands. Undaunted, the intrepid soldiers spliced the staff again and set it in place with the battle flag billowing again in the breeze. These soldiers were in full view of the enemy for about twelve minutes but never wavered in fulfilling their self-assigned mission. Elliott included this act of heroism in his daily report, naming the individual soldiers and their commands. It was another act of raw courage and served as a reminder to the Yankees that the fort's garrison still possessed a fighting spirit.[138] In December, General Beauregard rewarded their heroism by granting a twenty-day furlough to the private who initiated the action and furloughs of fifteen days for each of the other three soldiers who came to his assistance.

Elliott lost a valuable man on November 7, not from wounds, but from exhaustion. Captain John T. Champneys, who had arrived at Sumter in September along with Elliott to serve as the engineer in charge, asked to be relieved. Champneys's performance under dreadful conditions at Battery Wagner—where he had exhibited zeal, imagination and dedicated service—was highly commendable. His work at Sumter, despite the many challenges, was equally praiseworthy. It was under his supervision that recovery of Sumter proceeded so quickly. A Charleston newspaper described his departure with, "The two months of constant labor at the fort has somewhat affected the health of this officer, and he has been temporarily relieved, to recuperate, under medical advice."[139] Replacing him was another young captain of engineers, John Johnson, who would prove no less capable than his predecessor.

THE UNION BOMBARDMENT FROM Morris Island carried through the entire month of November, battering Sumter on a daily basis and often supported by the heavy guns of monitors and other warships. A total of 18,320 shells were fired at Sumter during the month, with 13,436 hits. Seven soldiers and five Negro laborers were killed by the enemy shells. Thirty-nine others, including ten Negroes, were wounded.[140] Yet, work inside the fort continued to enhance protection of the bomb-proof shelters sheltering the men, supplies and equipment while expanding the capabilities of the fort. Engineers and their work parties carried out a multitude of tasks amid the shelling on a daily basis, and Stephen Elliott worked to ensure that vigilance remained the byword of the garrison.

Interior of Fort Sumter in photograph from late 1863. *Library of Congress*.

Unbeknownst to anyone in Charleston, a series of events affecting Elliott took place in that month. Beauregard's November 6 message to President Davis urging more rank on behalf of Elliott apparently struck a chord, and on that same day, Davis sent an inquiry to the War Department regarding the status of Beauregard's promotion recommendation of September 9. The documentation and correspondence connected to it were found "pigeonholed, wrapped up in his father's application for a chaplainship."[141] Upon their retrieval, they were forwarded to Davis, who, upon returning from his trip to the Carolinas, reviewed them and, on November 17, directed the War

Department to promote Stephen Elliott to the rank of lieutenant colonel of artillery.[142] Beauregard's justifiable persistence paid off handsomely. The promotion was announced toward the end of the month, and the *Charleston Mercury* reported it on December 1 with praise and glee.

> *The brave Major Stephen Elliott has received his commission of a Lieutenant Colonel, and his promotion has been so richly merited as to give pleasure to many, the citizens of Charleston, and to the whole country. Advanced from a captaincy for gallant and meritorious services at the Battle of Pocotaligo in the fall of '62, his repulse of the attempted assault on Sumter from barges with a force of riflemen, and holding his post under this second severe and protracted bombardment, entitle him to the highest meed of praise. It is not unlikely that his unwearied energies and dauntless courage will receive more distinguished marks of favor from Richmond. They will be well won tributes of merit.*[143]

Mary Boykin Chesnut, a South Carolinian married to a Confederate general and famed for her wartime diary, entered this occasion in her journal. "Stephen Elliott is promoted, and who deserves it more.... [Her husband] lent them Sandy Hill; he would take no rent from a family doing their duty as were the Elliott's."[144]

The last day of November 1863 was notable, with only 24 shells fired at Sumter. The first five days of December recorded a total of just 443. Almost magically, none were fired the next three days. The forty-one-day barrage, termed the Second Great Bombardment, finally ended. Gillmore ordered a halt to the firing, because, as he saw it, the navy wasn't yet ready to attack Charleston, and he saw no need to continue bombarding the fort. Shortly afterward, Elliott's daily reports usually mentioned work being performed around the Morris Island batteries as the Yankees began adding to and strengthening them. Six shots were fired at Sumter on December 9, but the guns went silent again on the tenth.

Stephen Elliott Jr. as a lieutenant colonel. *Library of Congress.*

# CONFEDERATE GENERAL STEPHEN ELLIOTT

Unique image of Union shell exploding in Fort Sumter's interior, probably on December 9, 1863. *Library of Congress.*

Gillmore's stated reason to initiate the massive bombardment was to destroy the Three-Gun Battery. Yet, why he allowed the shelling to continue for nearly six weeks is unexplained. If he intended to break the will of the officers and men at Sumter, he failed miserably. Stephen Elliott, as well as Captains Champneys and Johnson and their engineering parties, remained unintimidated throughout this trying period. At the end, the fort was much stronger than it was at the start. Gillmore's continued interest in capturing the post is evident by the regular boat patrols testing the vigilance. The heavy reconnaissance in force of November 20, which had authorization to assault Sumter if it appeared lightly defended, clearly indicates that he held a lingering hope that the heavy bombardment had driven away most of the garrison, making it susceptible to capture. In the end, it was a test of wills between Gillmore and Beauregard. Gillmore's artillery power was countered by Beauregard's placement of superb leadership in Sumter, inspired and resolute at all levels, and Gillmore lost.

General Gillmore wrote numerous postwar articles about his experiences regarding Charleston and Fort Sumter. One of these is particularly interesting, as it belies his documented uninterrupted interest in taking Sumter in the fall of 1863. At the same time, the article credits the fort's garrison and acknowledges the added defensive measures put in place there.

> *The fort was destitute of cannon, could take no part in defense against a fleet, and as infantry outpost could be of no value. It was heroically held by the enemy in a spirit of commendable pride and audacity, and had been made very strong against capture by assault. The controlling conditions*

*differed essentially now, from those which obtained when the surrender of the place was demanded by the admiral early in September.*[145]

By December 1, Fort Sumter had set in place an elaborate system of interior defense. The primary defensive plan called for stopping any enemy assault at the walls, but Elliott called for a contingency plan to fall back on should, somehow, an enemy assault break through. In that event, the garrison would fall back into the bombproofs and casemates to provide close-in defense against the enemy within the fort while guns from Moultrie and other points opened up on Sumter, subjecting the attacking force, both outside and inside the fort, to intense bombardment. To bring this about, Elliott and his engineers devised barricades of logs and sandbags with firing slits for infantry and, in some sites, for the mountain howitzers. This truly was a plan of last resort but also one promising reasonable success. Elliott and everyone at the fort knew full well of Beauregard's intentions to hold the fort to the last extremity, and these imaginative measures certainly enhanced the ability to do it.[146]

THE REVEREND STEPHEN ELLIOTT Sr. tendered his resignation as an army chaplain on December 3. Citing his age, and that with five sons in the army he was the only male member of the family available to provide for his extended family, he was reluctantly resigning.[147]

MAJOR GENERAL J.F. GILMER, Beauregard's senior subordinate officer in Charleston, wrote a passionate letter to Richmond urging additional promotion for Lieutenant Colonel Elliott early in December. In it, Gilmer noted the favorable reports received from the many units who had served stints under Elliott at Fort Sumter and made special note of Elliott's reputation throughout the Charleston area.

> [Elliott's] *conduct since his assignment to the command has been such as to attract the attention, and receive the approbation, of all his superior officers, and to receive the full confidence and support of the whole garrison—officers and men—who have served under him. His energy, judgement, and coolness, under all circumstances have been such as to call forth the admiration of all the brave troops now engaged in the defense of Charleston.*[148]

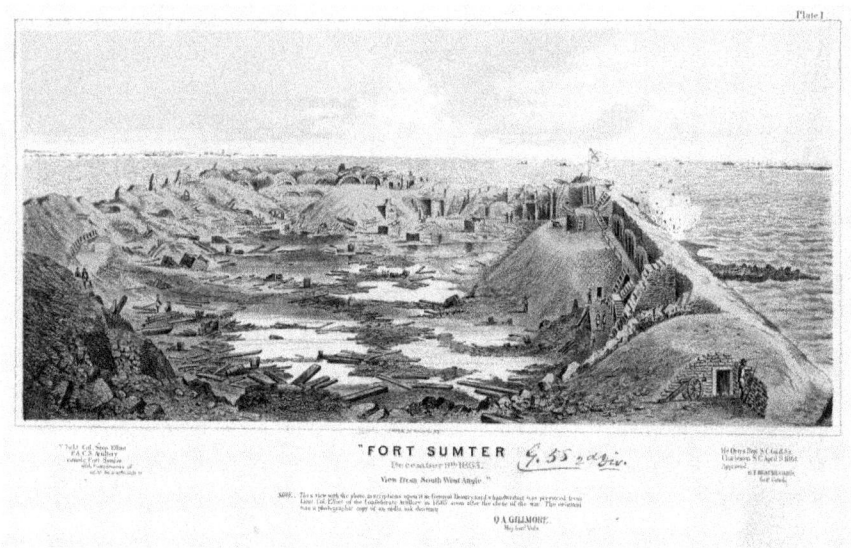

Fort Sumter, December 9, 1863. *Library of Congress.*

Tragedy struck without warning at Fort Sumter at 9:30 a.m. on December 11. The small-arms magazine with 150 pounds of black powder, located close to the fort's commissary where troops were standing in line for their rations, exploded, causing a massive fire within the bowels of the fort. The men close by were struck down by the concussion or consumed by the fiery blast. Stephen Elliott and his engineer in charge, Captain Johnson, asleep in their quarters after having spent most of the night on duty, were aroused by the noise of the explosion and smoke quickly filling their room. They quickly dressed, but frustrated by intense heat and thick smoke filling their casemate, the pair exited the fort through a shuttered embrasure, placing them on the outside of the fort amid much loose and dangerous rubble. After several minutes of treading a dangerous path taking them halfway around the fort, they succeeded in reentering the fort to find the garrison heroically fighting the flames and smoke, retrieving the dead and injured and rescuing others who were trapped.

Adding to the garrison's woes, Union artillery on Morris Island commenced bombarding the fort after noticing smoke rising from it. Though the Yankees had no idea what was happening at Sumter, the shelling continued for several hours with intentions of hindering the garrison in responding to an apparent emergency and to prevent assistance of any kind reaching the fort. In what was termed Sumter's "Second Minor Bombardment," 220 shots were fired on the fort during this day of distress, with just 33 missing.[149]

Shrapnel hit Elliott in the head and ankle, but he and the entire garrison continued valiantly to bring order out of chaos. Elliott was further frustrated when he learned that the fort's telegraph equipment was displaced and attempts by the Signal Corps personnel to reach other posts failed, leaving him cut off from outside communications for several hours. A small boat manned by brave sailors carrying water buckets made its way to the fort through the enemy shelling and assisted the garrison before retiring, carrying news of the calamity with them. Late that afternoon, telegraphic communications were reestablished, and Elliott was able to provide an early assessment of the situation at the fort. Fearful of an enemy assault, he also requested provisions, one hundred muskets, buckshot cartridges, fifty men, a set of telegraph equipment and two hundred yards of wire. Eleven men were killed and forty-one injured in the explosion, fire and shelling. All provisions were destroyed, and much of the garrison's blankets, clothing, weapons and accoutrements were lost to the flames. The fire remained out of control and spread to other areas before eventually burning itself out but leaving a staggering heat, preventing access to the magazine area for ten days.[150]

The next day, Elliott reported that "the damage done will not materially affect the defense of work. Captain Johnson, of the Engineers, was everywhere, doing everything that man could do." However, he severely castigated signal officers at other points who failed to respond to signals sent by Sumter during the crisis. He also acknowledged that, at one point in the night, his injuries "prevented him from running about" and he had to turn command of the fort over to his senior captain. Further, he acknowledged gratefully the prompt receipt of the men, rations, arms and ammunition he had requested.[151]

On the December 13, he tersely reported that the steamer did not arrive the previous night, leaving the garrison with no rations for the next day. While acknowledging that the weather was stormy, he pointed out that it didn't prevent guard and telegraph boats from arriving. He went further: "I am surprised that movements of importance should be left to the discretion and final decision of irresponsible and timid steamboat captains." That very night, Beauregard issued orders for an army officer to be put in charge of the supply boats on a temporary basis, and the next night, a steamer with a full load of rations and ordnance arrived.[152]

On December 14, Elliott wrote a letter to his family assuring them that he was fine and expected to continue fulfilling his duties at Sumter.

*My injuries are almost well. Those on my head entirely so, but I have to be careful about my foot on the rough ground which abounds here....I know that my position here* [Fort Sumter] *is an eyesore to some of my good friends but Gen'l B. placed me here and here I shall stay until he is ready to take me out or until I am taken to where there is rest....A man was killed stone dead within two feet of me... and I almost envied the poor fellow he dropped so quietly and easily and it actually seemed pleasantly.*[153]

This letter shows a determined and unshaken resolve to perform his assigned responsibilities while, at the same time, reflects how he had become accustomed to the attendant hardships of war. His mind remained clear and focused while his faith was unshaken after more than three months of arduous duty that few men could have handled so well.

General Beauregard visited the fort on the fifteenth to have a firsthand look at the damage and discuss the situation with Elliott and Captain Johnson. His report to Richmond the next day was positive and optimistic. "Inspected Sumter last night. Damage...less considerable than supposed; will soon be repaired. Colonel Elliott and garrison are confident, and in fine spirits. Sufficient bomb-proof still in good condition."[154] The cause of the explosion was never determined. Accordingly, no blame was placed on anyone for it, nor was there any reprimands issued. Repair efforts commenced immediately.

The fort garrison was completely replaced by the seventeenth, but the loss of so much interior space for quarters and storage was a major concern for some time to come. Duty at Sumter was to remain difficult until the fort's engineers were able to recover and rebuild some of the areas lost to the fire. Captain Johnson's record of events from December 12 to 31 is telling. "No firing upon the fort. The garrison much tried by labor and hardship of crowded quarters."[155]

CHRISTMAS 1863 WAS OBSERVED across the North and South in mostly peaceful conditions, but not in the city of Charleston, which had been on the receiving end of General Gillmore's long-range guns since August. At 1:00 a.m. on Christmas morning, Union guns on Morris Island opened a slow barrage on the city lasting until 1:12 p.m. A total of 149 huge shells were fired; 139 hit the city. One hit a building, causing a fire that engulfed five others and a cotton press. Seven civilians were injured, including an eighty-three-year-old man who had the lower part of a leg blown away by a shell bursting inside his home. His sister-in-law sustained a crushed foot. Both died of their injuries a few days later. The evening gun used to salute the flag being lowered on Morris Island fired a final shell at Charleston at sunset. There was no reprieve for Charleston that day.[156]

Most Confederate bastions came under fire on Christmas as well. At Fort Sumter, however, things were entirely different, with not a single shot fired at it. Further, Lieutenant Colonel Elliott, in conjunction with Beauregard's headquarters, had made arrangements for the garrison to mark the occasion as best it could with a proper Christmas meal provided in the confines of the Three-Gun Battery. Using a cannon chassis as the table, sandbags and artillery shells as chairs and half of a huge mortar shell serving as a punch bowl, a feast far beyond the normal rations was served, with fare including roast turkey, ducks, oysters, sweet potatoes and other delicacies, all of which were a delight to men who had not seen such food in a long while.[157]

Sketch showing a view of the southeast angle at Fort Sumter in December 1863. *Library of Congress.*

December 31 was another day of moderate or light shelling at posts around Charleston but free of shelling for Sumter. However, something stunning and far out of the ordinary happened at the fort. The daily journal of events maintained by Beauregard's staff included specific mention of Elliott's daily report from that day. "About sunset the enemy fired 2 shots over Fort Sumter and, at the report of the evening gun from the latter work [Sumter], the Federal flag on Morris Island was dipped in salute. This unusual and unexpected piece of courtesy on the part of the Yankees is deemed worthy of record."[158]

From this short report, it is clear that the Yankees intentionally fired the two shots *over* the fort, not at it, to garner the fort's attention for their flag salute, which came shortly afterward. What prompted this profound courtesy—a formal and clear sign of respect—cannot be stated with certainty, but the act itself could only have been authorized at the highest level of the Union command. It simply had to be General Gillmore's way of saluting the noble fort itself and its resolute commander, Lieutenant Colonel Stephen Elliott, for gallantly enduring so much for so long.

The 142 days from August 12, the date of the first firing on Sumter by Gillmore's rifled artillery, through December 31 had been hellish. On exactly one half of those days, Gillmore's massive guns, along with those of the Union navy, bombarded the fort, firing a total 26,767 shells registering 19,738 hits. In all, 43 men, including 5 Negro workmen, were killed in this time, and an additional 165, 23 of them Negroes, were injured. The fort's structure no longer resembled its 1861 appearance, but the Confederate flag still waved on the sea breezes above it, and the men within its confines remained determined to hold it.

# 6

# POST OF HONOR: FORT SUMTER (JANUARY–APRIL 1864)

January 1864 saw the major Confederate and Union armies alike in winter quarters recovering from the bloody and savage battles of the previous year while preparing for the new ones expected in the spring. The South knew that the North would likely initiate new offensives in Virginia and elsewhere and expected 1864 to be the deciding year of the war. Wearied from nearly three years of warfare filled with massive casualties, both sides were very much aware that U.S. president Abraham Lincoln faced reelection in the fall and the results of the ballot, rather than the bullet, might be the deciding factor on how the war would ultimately be settled. If he was defeated, a negotiated peace would likely occur. Until then, for the South, a strong defensive posture must be maintained. For the North, a powerful and successful offensive was the only option.

At Fort Sumter, the new year began as the old one had ended. Engineering work continued toward improving quarters for the garrison, enemy fleet activities off Charleston's harbor and activities on Morris Island were reported and vigilance against enemy small-boat attacks was maintained. Just after 4:00 a.m. on January 4, the fort received a warning from the navy's guard boat that a pair of small boats and a monitor were approaching. Because the night was foggy and ripe for an assault, Elliott had his garrison on the alert and prepared for action. No attack occurred that night, but the next night, with another thick fog and calm sea conditions, Elliott saw conditions favorable for the enemy boats and "multiplied sentinels by 10."[159] On January 14, he reported his concerns about an assault: "The density of the fog affords good cause for an assault, but it would not find us unprepared."[160] No assaults were made, but their potential threat never subsided in the minds of Elliott or his garrison.

On January 20, Stephen Elliott took a weeklong furlough. Other than having been called to Charleston for a few hours at a time on a couple of occasions for official business, this was his first opportunity to relax in over four months. With no enemy shelling and having a capable senior captain of the fort—F.T. Miles of the Twenty-Seventh South Carolina infantry—the opportunity for the furlough was one of perfect timing. General Beauregard probably had little hesitation in granting Elliott's request for the furlough.[161] Little happened in Elliott's absence other than that the water boat failed to arrive on consecutive nights.[162]

Elliott returned the night of January 27 and found the engineering work progressing nicely. However, the peace and tranquility at Sumter soon ended. At 9:00 on the night of January 28, enemy guns and mortars began a heavy fire on the fort, causing Elliott to order the steamer, full of supplies and equipment, to depart when only partially offloaded. Shelling continued at an irregular basis through the thirty-first, when it ended as abruptly as it had begun. In what was termed the "Third Minor Bombardment," almost six hundred shells were fired at the fort but caused little damage and few casualties.[163]

The shelling sparked another display of gallantry by members of the garrison when, on January 30, the flagstaff was shot away. Elliott reported it in detail.

> *At 3 p.m. the flag staff was shot down; it was first replaced upon a small and afterwards a larger staff by Private F. Schafer…who stood upon the top of the traverse and repeatedly waved the flag in sight of the enemy. He was assisted by* [three others]. *They were exposed to a rapid and accurate fire of shells. At the close of the scene Schafer, springing from a cloud of smoke and dust of a burning shell, stood long waving his hat in triumph. It was a most gallant deed, and the effect on the garrison was most inspiring.*[164]

February was relatively quiet, with sporadic interruptions by enemy shell fire sixteen days of the month. Only once did Elliott mention in his reports enemy boats coming near the fort. On January 23, he advised Beauregard, "Two of the enemy's picket-boats approached within 500 yards last night. If they return tonight, I will open on them with the boat howitzer."[165] It was

Sketch of Fort Sumter's interior by Confederate engineer officer in 1864. *Library of Congress.*

obvious that he and his garrison maintained a tight vigil despite the respite from heavy bombardment.

A major accomplishment was reached on January 12, when the last of three additional heavy guns was placed at Sumter, bringing the total of mounted cannon to six.[166] This feat climaxed a long-term effort by Elliott and Captain Johnson with his engineers in which they slowly overcame numerous obstacles, difficulties and temporary setbacks. Bombproofs had been enlarged and quarters expanded, allowing for more protection and comfort for the garrison. Imagination, skill, hard work and determination by those involved made this happen.

February held another special day at Fort Sumter. In both the North and the South, it was traditional to celebrate the twenty-second of the month in a festive manner in commemoration of George Washington's birthday, and

Elliott ensured that it was duly observed. A Charleston newspaper carried a lengthy description of the observance at Sumter. The Charleston Light Infantry and the Eutaw Band came to the fort and were prominent in the festivities. The program of the day, carefully detailed in the newspaper, called for toasts to President Washington, the Commandant of Fort Sumter (Lieutenant Colonel Elliott), the Engineer Corps of Fort Sumter, the Medical Corps at the fort, Departed Comrades and the Women of the South. Following each toast, the band played appropriate music. Elliott and Engineer Captain Johnson each gave responses to the audience following their toasts. The song selected for Elliott was "Hail to the Chief," and that for Johnson was "Root Hog or Die," a song attesting to the rewards of hard work and popular among the armies of both the North and South. A moment of silence followed by "Rest, Spirit, Rest" followed the toast to the "Departed Comrades." The program contained eloquent tributes to all who were toasted. Elliott's read, "His chivalric bearing and soldierly demeanor justly entitle him to the confidence and esteem of his countrymen." Songs by the glee club concluded the day's celebration.[167]

The most serious difficulty Elliott faced in the month was on February 29, when sixteen soldiers declined to answer to their names at muster. For some reason, they thought that doing so would automatically reenlist them under proposed regulations of the War Department. Elliott showed great patience in this matter but could not completely resolve it. Reporting the details of the matter to Beauregard, he wrote: "they do not refuse to do duty.…If there are any orders on the subject please send them down by tonight's boat."[168] That the men continued to do their duty appears to have been sufficient to satisfy Elliott that he could allow this administrative matter to be settled later as long as it did not adversely affect security of Sumter nor cause dissension and turmoil with other troops. Certainly, had he felt their actions were a mutiny or adverse to the fort's morale, he would have caused them to be arrested and shipped from Sumter immediately. Apparently, Beauregard left matters to Elliott's discretion and the situation never worsened, for there is no further mention of it in any of Elliott's correspondence.

MARCH 1864 WAS VERY similar to February. Occasional shelling from Union guns on Morris Island took place but caused little damage. However, on March 15, the enemy ramped up their fire on Sumter with the "Fourth Minor Bombardment," lasting from 10:30 in the morning until sunset. A total of 143 shots were fired at Sumter, and 100 of them hit. Not a single mention of enemy boats nearing the fort is found in Elliott's reports for this month.

However, important events were taking place elsewhere. In Washington, President Lincoln nominated U.S. Grant as general-in-chief of the U.S. Army, and Grant immediately announced that his headquarters were to be in the field, with the U.S. Army of the Potomac facing the Confederate Army of Northern Virginia under Robert E. Lee. Grant and his staff began making plans for a spring offensive intended to destroy Lee's army, take Richmond and end the war. Neither Stephen Elliott nor his commander, General P.G.T. Beauregard, had any inkling of how this would affect them in the coming weeks.

April 1864 brought twelve days of shelling of Sumter, some of them quite heavy. On April 13, Elliott requested and received permission from General Beauregard to fire a thirteen-gun salute in honor of the 1861 capture of Fort Sumter by the Confederacy. The next day, at noon, his signal gun fired the commemorative salute.[169] The Fifth Minor Bombardment began on April 28 and ended on May 4 after 510 shells were fired on Sumter. Captain Johnson and his engineers, despite the shelling, extended their progress in making Sumter more formidable. Stephen Elliott took another furlough from April 15 to 25 and, after inspecting the fort following his return, expressed pleasure with the progress made in his absence.[170]

An unexpected and major change in Charleston's command structure occurred while Elliott was on his well-deserved furlough. General Beauregard relinquished command upon receipt of orders taking him to Virginia to command a military department stretching from the south side of the James River below Richmond well into North Carolina. The general's twenty-month service in Charleston was extraordinary and highly creditable in every way. Authorities in Richmond, anticipating that Grant's huge army in Virginia was about to begin its long-awaited campaign, felt Beauregard's talents, skills and ability were needed more in Virginia than in Charleston. On April 20, General Beauregard was relieved by General Sam Jones. This change in command was only the first of a series of changes ultimately affecting Stephen Elliott.

# 7
# ON TO VIRGINIA (MAY–JUNE 1864)

On May 1, General Quincy Gillmore relinquished command in Charleston and headed to Fortress Monroe in Virginia, where he was named a corps commander in the newly formed Army of the James under General Benjamin "the Beast" Butler. Many Union troops were withdrawn from Charleston, Beaufort and other posts along the South Atlantic coastline at the same time to serve in Virginia.

In Charleston, Confederate general Nathan G. Evans was making ready to take his brigade to Virginia to serve in General Beauregard's department when he incurred serious injuries in a buggy accident on April 23. This unfortunate accident led to a quick search for a replacement. Beauregard flexed his muscles by quickly registering his preference for General William S. Walker, hero of Pocotaligo in 1862 who had recently transferred to a command post in Kinston, North Carolina. Beauregard held Evans in disdain. Among the reasons for it was his familiarity with the brigade while it was serving in Charleston. A much-publicized feud between Evans and some of his regimental commanders resulted in proceedings adversely affecting the reputations of all the officers involved in the feud. Additionally, a close inspection of the brigade found it deficient in many respects, with most being blamed on poor leadership. Though the brigade had battle-experienced colonels, Beauregard felt it needed a commander with the ability to bring about positive changes, including the increasing of morale. His past experience with General Walker was excellent in every regard, and Walker's fine record of service made this selection easy for him. The

War Department acceded to Beauregard's request by appointing Walker to command the brigade on the twenty-ninth and ordering him to Virginia with Beauregard. At the same time, the Holcombe Legion infantry regiment, part of Evan's (now Walker's) brigade, lacked a colonel. This was resolved by the War Department when, on April 20, it promoted Stephen Elliott to full colonel and named him commanding officer of the legion. There was no quibbling this time about whether an artillery officer could be promoted to the command of an infantry regiment. Elliott's superb command of Fort Sumter, an infantry post, and the accolades received were more than sufficient to justify this promotion. The outcome of this unique set of circumstances meant that Elliott would be reunited with Generals Walker and Beauregard and, once again, be facing General Gillmore.

Elliott knew nothing of the pending promotion and was caught totally off guard on learning of it on May 2. That night, he wrote his wife, Charlotte, a letter and, for once, openly showed his innermost thoughts.

> *I was thinking how tired of the fort I was and wondering how and when I would get out of it when a member of the Signal Corps stepped up and informed me that I was appointed Col. of the Holcombe Legion Infantry. I was and am glad and have not hesitated a single second about accepting. The Legion is in General Walker's Brigade....I have not yet heard when I am to be relieved but my commission directs me to report to General Beauregard....You need not bother yourself about my being shot. I have been shelled down here until I am perfectly sick of it.*[171]

His letter closed on a light-hearted note lamenting the need for "a good cook I must have or my 'innards' will cave. I do not mean a French cook but one who can boil hominy done and cook biscuits."[172] The new assignment certainly uplifted his spirits and gave hope for the future. The *Charleston Mercury* published a worthy acknowledgement the next day. "Our readers will be glad to learn that the gallant and accomplished commander of Fort Sumter has just been promoted to the rank of full Colonel—his commission to date from the 20th ult. Colonel Elliott, as we hear, is assigned to command the Holcombe Legion. A worthy leader of so fine a body of troops."[173]

Elliott's last day in command of Fort Sumter was May 4, and he left Charleston shortly afterward to catch up with the Holcombe Legion, already in Virginia. His departure was marked by news that U.S. Grant's spring offensive in Virginia had commenced and Lee was moving his army to meet them. Over the next few days, the two armies would be locked in bloody battles at The Wilderness and Spotsylvania Court House. At the same time, Benjamin Butler's Army of the James sailed up the James River, took City Point (now Hopewell, Virginia) and moved toward Richmond, starting what became known as the Bermuda Hundred Campaign.

On the eleventh, Elliott wrote his wife a letter describing his new situation. The pace he now faced was far more hectic than he was used to. Though his regiment was spread out guarding bridges at three locations (Stoney Creek, Jarratt's Station and Nottoway Bridge) well below Petersburg and far from the rest of Walker's Brigade, he had met with the men of the regiment and come away feeling it was composed of "excellent material." Other personal observations were that his quarters in Stoney Creek were in a house with a single intact chair and that he was having difficulty adjusting to the lack of coffee. On a positive note, he suggested the possibility of having her come to him.[174] Undoubtedly, he followed news from the front closely and with a watchful eye, knowing that his brother Ralph was in the terrible battles above Richmond.

The fighting above Richmond continued with high intensity and with no sign of diminishing, as the armies of Lee and Grant remained locked in a bitter struggle. At Petersburg, General Butler had failed miserably in carrying out his assignment of moving northward to take Richmond while Lee was occupied with Grant. Desperate stands by outnumbered Confederates kept the timid Butler at bay in the comparatively small but intense engagements of Port Walthall Junction, Swift Creek and Chester Station, less than a dozen miles below Richmond. Beauregard's arrival with reinforcements strengthened the Confederate hand, but the situation remained fluid and intense for several more days with a series of additional engagements.

May 20 was a pivotal day in the Bermuda Hundred Campaign. Beauregard came within a whisker of destroying a large portion of Butler's army at the Battle of Ware Bottom Church, the eighth and final engagement of the fourteen-day campaign. A brilliant plan executed well was foiled when one of his subordinate generals made an inexcusable error. Still, Butler was forced to withdraw to his main line of defense, allowing Beauregard to bottle him up and emphatically end Butler's hopes of taking Richmond, thus relieving pressure on Lee, who was still locked in battle to the north of Richmond. Beauregard's superb leadership in a critical time was decisive. Toward the end of the battle, something happened that would have a major impact on Stephen Elliott. General William Walker, leading the bulk of his brigade in extended action, was wounded and captured by the Yankees. He was taken to the rear, where Union surgeons amputated the lower part of a leg but saved his life. Walker's Brigade was now without a commanding general.

Elliott's letter from Stoney Creek to Charlotte on May 22 gives more description of his surroundings, notes he had been to Petersburg and assures her that his post was quite strong. He also related a puzzling, hurried surprise visit by a major from General Braxton Bragg's staff who "asked about twenty questions in three minutes and wrote down my answers on the back of a letter." In the same letter, he laments that he has "not heard a word of Ralph."[175]

The reason for the strange visit by Bragg's staff officer became vividly clear on May 29, when Elliott received a telegram informing him he was promoted to brigadier general. General Beauregard again chose to use his influence in filling this position by requesting that Stephen Elliott, the most junior colonel in the brigade, be appointed its commanding officer over its more seasoned regimental commanders. This unusual request was far out of normal military protocol, but Beauregard's desire to have a solid leader in possession of an unblemished record and sterling reputation prevailed. It is certain the War Department was already working on considering Elliott for the position, for the records show his appointment to that rank occurred on May 24, 1864. Beauregard's official request for Elliott's promotion is dated May 25. "The capture of Brig. Gen. Walker and amputation of his foot leaves his brigade without a proper commander. It is necessary for the good of the service that a competent Brigadier should be appointed to its command immediately. I beg to recommend for that position Col. Stephen Elliott now Colonel of the Holcombe Legion belonging to the same brigade."[176]

The War Department wasted little time on Elliott's status, and the appointment was confirmed May 28, with Elliott being advised the next day. The brief interview and questioning he underwent were obviously formalities to assess his military qualifications on behalf of certain authorities in the War Department. On May 30, he wrote his wife about the promotion.

> *I received a telegram yesterday afternoon announcing the startling fact that I have been made Brigadier and would take command of Walker's Brigade at once. I was very much startled at first but…my first impressions were full of misgivings lest I should be all unprepared for so grand a responsibility. After seeking guidance where it is always to be found I felt more assured.…I left for Petersburg at midnight…and arrived at daylight. After taking a little nap, I* [visited] *General Beauregard.*[177]

His brigade, now called "Elliott's Brigade," consisted of the Holcombe Legion Infantry and the Seventeenth, Eighteenth, Twenty-Second, Twenty-Third and Twenty-Sixth South Carolina Infantry Regiments and was attached to Major General Bushrod Johnson's division. Affectionately known as the "Tramp Brigade," the regiments had served well together through many actions. It took its nickname from the fact that it seemed to always be "tramping" and on the move, with assignments in Virginia, Georgia, both Carolinas and Mississippi. Elliott wrote in a letter to his wife on June 1 that he had tried to call on General Johnson but missed him that day. He added that he did find Beauregard and had a long talk.[178] He soon met General Johnson and described his first impression of him in an undated letter to his wife, using some of his sailing terms: "Bushrod Johnson is a good old fellow, a good hard fighter and an honest man., but carries very little sail, steers badly."[179] The brigade, minus the Holcombe Legion, had performed well on May 20 in the Battle of Ware Bottom Church, and Elliott joined it in place along the Confederate Howlett Line, keeping Butler's Army of the James bottled up in the Bermuda Hundred.

IN THE MEANTIME, ABOVE Richmond, Grant continued his relentless attacks on Lee's army, resulting in tremendous casualties on both sides. On June 1, he began moving his army toward a site named Cold Harbor, where he hoped to achieve a breakthrough. On that day, several small but heated engagements occurred, and in one of them, Captain Ralph Elliott, Stephen's brother, was severely wounded. Taken to a hospital in Richmond, Ralph lingered until dying on June 5.[180] He was buried without fanfare in a nearby cemetery holding many other Confederate soldiers who also paid the ultimate price in defense of their country.

Stephen Elliott narrowly missed being tested as a brigade commander on June 2 when Beauregard ordered a reconnaissance in force to test the Union defenses opposite the Howlett Line. Elliott's brigade was one of three thrown forward for this purpose. Driving in Union pickets, the Confederate advance gained momentum, pushing several enemy regiments away before being stopped by heavy artillery fire from the main defensive works. Though some of the ground gained was lost later to Union counterattacks, the Yankee picket lines were now forced much closer to their main line of fortifications. Elliott's brigade again performed well, even though he arrived too late to be involved.

The next day, Grant hurled his army against Lee's in an ill-fated assault at Cold Harbor, incurring over seven thousand casualties in less than half an hour. The attack against the dug-in and determined Confederate Army of Northern Virginia was a total disaster for the Union commander, and his offensive operations were brought to a screeching halt. Over the next week, he anguished about his next move. Ultimately, he decided to build a pontoon bridge over the wide James River, cross his army over it and advance on lightly defended Petersburg, just twenty miles below Richmond. If he could take Petersburg before Lee had time to shift his army southward, then Lee and Richmond would be cut off from their primary supply lines. The plan was daring and imaginative and one that should have worked.

On June 9, Union general Benjamin Butler, with almost five thousand men, attacked Beauregard and his twenty-five hundred Confederates at Petersburg but was driven back after desperate fighting. Meanwhile, Grant's plans to shift his operation south of the James River were being prepared and put in place. On June 15, two corps of Grant's army, about eighteen thousand men across the James and Appomattox Rivers, were beginning their advance on the outer defensive works of Petersburg. Delays and confusion of all sorts muddled any hope of an immediate assault that morning. When finally ready late in the afternoon, the Yankees achieved substantial success against the undermanned Confederates. Petersburg was actually open to be taken that evening, but a fateful decision by the Yankee commanders, one of them General Quincy Gillmore, to postpone further advances until the next morning doomed them.

That same day. Elliott wrote his beloved wife a lengthy letter fully sharing his thoughts. In one part, he cheerfully teased her about receiving her last two letters addressed to "Col. E." and gently reminded her that she was the wife of a brigadier general. Much of the letter, however, was focused on his outlook toward commanding the brigade.

> *I have read and studied all that I think absolutely necessary for the handling of the brigade in the field and for the rest I must rely on providence giving me power to use my common sense as the occasion demands....I hope that my first fight may be conducted under commands of some superior officer leaving me only the execution of what he orders....I earnestly by night comfort myself at the guidance of God and whatever appears to be my duty I do it.*[181]

# CONFEDERATE GENERAL STEPHEN ELLIOTT

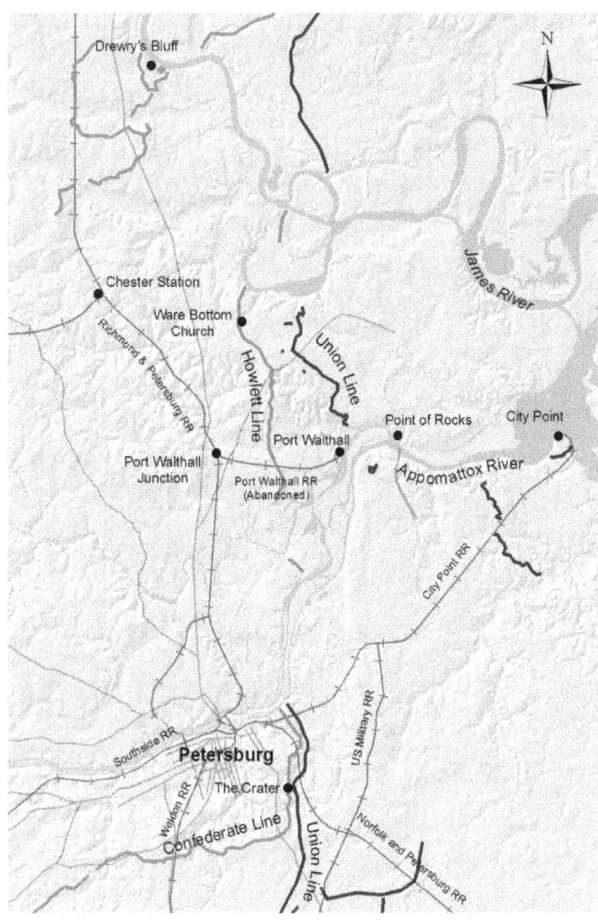

Map showing 1864 Confederate positions at Bermuda Hundred and Petersburg, Virginia. *Courtesy of Scott Williams and the Chesterfield Historical Society of Virginia.*

June 15 was a terrible day for General Beauregard, who frantically sought reinforcements. Neither Robert E. Lee nor the War Department in Richmond believed that Grant had crossed the James and refused to send him any troops. In a desperate move to hold Petersburg, Beauregard ordered Bushrod Johnson's division to abandon the Howlett Line, about ten miles away, and hasten to him at Petersburg early on the morning of June 16. With other reinforcements from elsewhere, Beauregard now had about nine thousand men, but to his front were about fifty-three thousand Union soldiers, with the rest of Grant's massive army across the James and coming toward him. Grant's masterly move completely eluded Lee, and Petersburg, its vital railroads and Richmond were almost in his grasp.

But two things took place that day to completely foil Grant's ambitions. The on-scene Union commanders again dawdled, and the scheduled morning assault was delayed until after 5:00 in the afternoon. In that brief period, Beauregard had his men feverishly prepared defensive lines and positions to receive the anticipated attack. Tensions were high on the Confederate side, but Beauregard's leadership under the most desperate circumstances paid off when the enemy assault began. Intense fighting took place along the newly formed lines lasting for over three hours and ending only after darkness set in. Despite the odds in their favor, the enemy made only modest gains that day. The next morning, the Yankees again attacked, making limited progress through several major assaults and sustaining heavy casualties in fighting that ended about midnight. That night, Beauregard pulled his men back to a new defensive line for which the men had to prepare new positions. New trenches had to be dug by men nearly exhausted, but without murmur they put their shovels, axes and whatever other implements they possessed to good use, knowing full well the enemy would renew battle the next day.

General Robert E. Lee had finally been convinced that Grant's army was no longer to his front north of the James but was now threatening Petersburg. He reacted firmly and quickly, beginning a flow of welcomed reinforcements to Beauregard. Two full divisions of troops arrived the morning of June 18, and Lee arrived just before noon. Several Union assaults were made throughout the day, each easily repulsed. Later that afternoon, the balance of Lee's Army of Northern Virginia arrived and was placed in position. By the end of the day, it was apparent to Union commanders that they could not accomplish their goals. With great regret, they began digging in. Thus ended the Second Battle of Petersburg, and the Siege of Petersburg began.

Beauregard once again had displayed incredible and inspirational leadership in time of crisis. Bushrod Johnson's division was prominent in the fighting from June 16 to 18. With little rest or food between resisting assaults and perfecting their defensive positions, Stephen Elliott and his brigade of veterans performed well in meeting the extended and unexpected challenge of the difficult situation they were thrown into. That they had been in the thick of things is evidenced by the fact that Elliott himself was struck by spent balls or shrapnel four times on the seventeenth.[182] The *Richmond Daily Dispatch* noted more severe action next day. "The enemy made several severe demonstrations during the day on different portions of our lines, but were in every instance repulsed with loss. In the evening the Yankees advanced in several lines of battle in front of Elliott's brigade, and when they were within four hundred yards our troops opened on them with grape and canister, mowing down hundreds at every discharge."[183]

# 8

# PETERSBURG AND THE CRATER (JULY–AUGUST 1864)

The next several weeks found the armies of both sides entrenching outside Petersburg. Though there were no assaults, there were daily casualties from occasional shelling and the fire of sharpshooters. Johnson's division remained busy enhancing their position and building other defensive works to their rear. Additionally, some men were assigned the task of recovering unexploded ordnance and lead from spent musket fire. Johnson required one-third of his men to be awake at all times and the entire division to be under arms at 2:00 a.m. each morning. Duty in the trenches was not easy in the summer heat. Elliott's Brigade received a rare reprieve by being relieved from the works on July 11 but were returned to the same site three days later.[184] Their duty in the trenches can only be described as hot, tiring and dangerous.

The Yankees were facing many of the same frustrations, dangers and exertions as the Confederates. Slowly, entrenchments were extended in a generally southward direction, with placements made for artillery batteries. One work detail, however, was unique to the Yankees. On June 25, work began toward construction of a mine running from Union lines to a Confederate position over five hundred feet away across a small hollow. The targeted position was the salient extending somewhat outward from the Confederate line and manned by Elliott's Brigade. The concept was that the mine would be packed with sufficient black powder under the salient to blow a huge opening in the Confederate position, thus allowing infantry to push forward from Union positions and enter the opening unmolested and in sufficient force to spread out and capture Petersburg.

Rumors of the mining somehow quickly spread, and over the next month, Northern newspapers mentioned it on a regular basis. Union soldiers taunted their Southern counterparts with comments referring to an underground explosion. Confederate engineers were called in to conduct countermining efforts in an attempt to detect and confirm any such threat. Confederate engineers took steps to ensure that particular part of the line would remain defensible if such a mine was used by building more entrenchments to the rear of the salient and placing mortars and artillery within range. Meanwhile, Elliott and his brigade went about their daily duties. The mine was completed on July 23 without interruption or detection. A few days later, four tons of black powder were stacked and packed by the Yankees twenty feet below the ground directly under Elliott's salient. Plans for the attack were made, revised and only formalized late on July 29 for an attack the next morning.

About 4:55 a.m. on Saturday, July 30, the black powder in the mine exploded with a devastating force, rending the earth above in a gigantic upheaval. Men, cannon and anything else in its way were hurled skyward like toys. In an instant, Confederate works above and around it were obliterated as the earth flew upward from the force of the blast and then fell back to earth. Stephen Elliott, awakened immediately by the roar and trembling of the earth, rushed from his bombproof to see the horror of the explosion through the thick smoke and dust and the moans of the injured. His quick investigation showed that most of two of his regiments, the Eighteenth and Twenty-Second, were caught up in the blast and either killed or incapacitated. Additionally, Peagram's nearby four-gun battery lost two cannon and most of its men. The crater left by the blast measured "135 feet in length, 97 feet in breadth, and 30 feet deep."[185]

The Union assault was delayed and hampered in getting underway about fifteen minutes after the explosion and, on reaching the crater, stopped. The loose dirt of the crater and accurate fire from nearby Confederate positions hindered the leading elements in climbing to the top, and within another fifteen minutes, it was packed with troops unable to go forward. Poor Union leadership led to further problems. The commanding generals elected to remain in Union lines, causing the attack to suffer for lack of on-scene leadership and coordination.

Elliott, however, showed remarkable coolness and soundness in his reactions to the disaster and began implementation of the contingency plan formulated for exactly this situation. Gathering the commanders of two of his remaining regiments, he quickly began issuing the necessary orders. The situation is best described by Colonel F.W. McMaster, commanding the Seventeenth South Carolina during the battle, who described it vividly in an 1899 letter published in a South Carolina newspaper.

> *Gen. Stephen Elliott, the hero of Fort Sumter a fine gentleman and a superb officer, came up soon after the explosion. He was dressed in a new uniform, and looked like a game cock. He surveyed the scene for a few minutes, he disappeared and in a short time he came up to me accompanied by Col. A.R. Smith, of the Twenty-Sixth South Carolina, with a few men, who were working their way through the crowd. He said to me, "Colonel, I am going to charge these Yankees out of the crater, you follow Smith with your regiment." He immediately climbed the counterscarp. The gallant Smith followed and about a half dozen men followed. And in less than five minutes he was shot that day from the northern side of the crater. He was immediately pulled down into the ditch, and with utmost coolness, and no exhibition of pain turned the command over to me, the next ranking officer.*[186]

General Bushrod Johnson's after-action report noted Elliott's initial steps in a complimentary manner.

> *Brig. Gen. S. Elliott, the gallant commander of the brigade which occupied the salient, was making prompt disposition of his forces to assault the enemy and reoccupy the portion of the trench...when he was dangerously wounded. He had given the necessary orders for* [McMaster's and Smith's regiments] *to be withdrawn from the trenches and preceded them to the open ground...when he was struck by a rifle-ball.*[187]

Stephen Elliott was hit by a bullet that struck his left arm and penetrated his chest, passing through his lung. Taken to the rear by men around him, his personal involvement in the Battle of the Crater at Elliott's Salient ended less than an hour after it commenced. His brigade, however, won much acclaim that fateful day, for it held a portion of crater rim until reinforcements arrived and, after nearly five hours of continuous fighting, assisted in driving the enemy away. The brigade's conspicuous and heroic stand was vital to the Confederate victory and, unfortunately, is often overlooked by historians. Nearly four thousand Yankees were killed, wounded or captured that day in another stunning defeat for Grant. Again, he saw a well-devised plan thwarted by his determined and well-led counterparts in gray. Confederate casualties totaled about fifteen hundred men, with seven hundred of them from Elliott's Brigade.

Sent to a nearby Petersburg hospital while the fighting progressed,

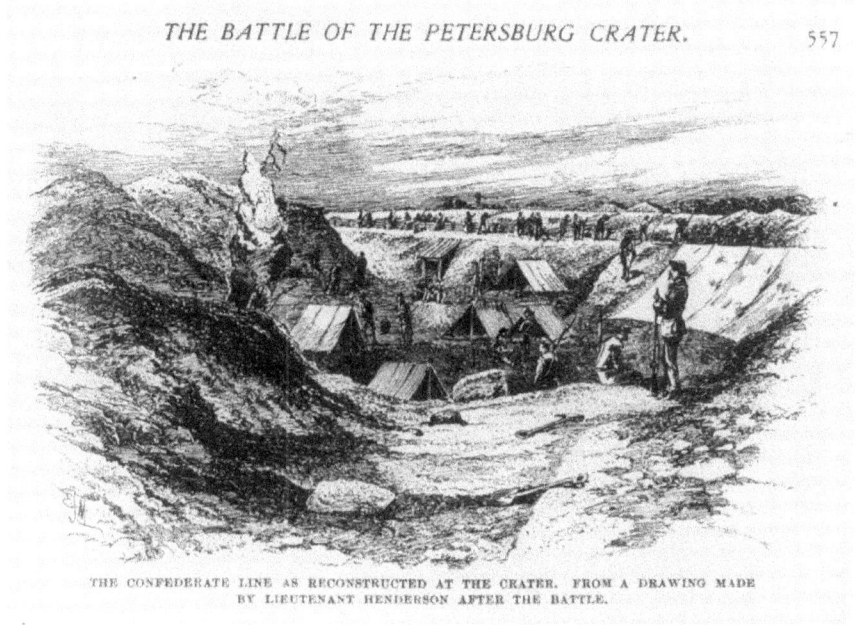

Wartime sketch by a Confederate officer of The Crater at Petersburg after the battle and with the Confederate line reestablished. *Library of Congress.*

Elliott was quickly examined by surgeons, who first declared the wounds as mortal.[188] News of his wounding and its seriousness was sent to Elliott's family. Mary Boykin Chesnut noted this in her famous diary with: "Stephen Elliott is wounded. His wife and father have gone to him."[189] He languished in the Petersburg hospital but, surprisingly, showed signs of improvement right away. A Charleston newspaper reported on August 11: "A dispatch from the venerable father of General Elliott to a friend in the city, brings the following gratifying intelligence, 'General Elliott is rapidly improving'."[190] His father's report was not just wishful hoping, for, on August 18, Elliott was deemed by the surgeons to be sufficiently strong enough for a furlough of thirty days.[191]

## 9

# THE FINAL CAMPAIGN (SEPTEMBER 1864–APRIL 1865)

Few records are found tracing Elliott's whereabouts for the next couple of months. His wounds definitely left him in a weakened state, as attested to by a report from the Board of Examiners for Furloughs and Discharges (a medical command) in Columbia, South Carolina, dated November 1, 1864. "The Board hereby certify that it has carefully examined this officer and find that he is suffering from gun shot wound of left arm with complete paralysis…and that in consequences thereof he is, in the opinion of the Board, unfit for duty. It further declares its belief that he will not be able to resume duties in a less period than sixty days."[192]

The *Charleston Mercury* noted his brief presence in Charleston in an article dated November 19. "Gen. Stephen Elliott, now convalescent, passed through the city yesterday, en route for Savannah. We regret to learn the General has nearly lost the use of his left arm."[193] He was never to regain full use of the arm.

During the period between Elliott's wounding and his Charleston visit, the war had gone badly for the Confederacy. In Virginia, the siege of Petersburg continued unabated with sharp, vicious battles stretching from the outskirts of Richmond to well below Petersburg. Grant continually extended his lines, threatening the city and the railroad supply lines. Robert E. Lee and his valiant Army of Northern Virginia contested the enemy time and time again. Elliott's Brigade, now commanded by someone else, marched and fought several engagements.

## BEAUFORT LEGEND, CHARLESTON HERO

In the West, Confederate general Joseph Johnston squared off against Union general W.T. Sherman, who, on May 1, 1864, set his huge army in motion from Chattanooga with intentions of taking Atlanta, Georgia, about 115 miles away. Numerous major and minor engagements followed through the summer, and though his progress was slow, Sherman kept making headway, steadily inching closer to the city. With Grant stymied at Petersburg, the eyes of both the North and South were focused on Sherman and Johnston over the summer. On September 2, 125 days after his campaign commenced, Sherman victoriously entered Atlanta. The loss of Atlanta depleted the South's hopes while boosting those of the North. It gave Abraham Lincoln badly needed momentum in his campaign for reelection against former Union general George B. McClellan, who favored a negotiated peace with the Confederacy and an end to the war. When the ballots were cast on November 8, Lincoln won 2.1 million popular votes against McClellan's 1.8 million, and both sides now knew that the war would continue without pause.

Sherman stayed in Atlanta until a week after Lincoln's reelection, when, after burning the city, he started his infamous "March to the Sea" with the goal of taking Savannah, Georgia. With no Confederate force of any size in his path, he had only to contend with Georgia militia and Confederate general Joseph Wheeler's cavalry for the 240-mile journey. His army progressed at a slow clip toward Savannah and, unworried about interference, burned farms, towns, villages, mills, storehouses, churches, courthouses and all manner of dwellings in a 60-mile wide swath. The Yankee army looted anything that could be carried from homes of citizens and destroyed the rest while committing horrible crimes, including rape and murder, against defenseless civilians. Young and old, male and female, white and black, all suffered horribly from the unprecedented cruelty of Sherman's men. Food and livestock not taken to supply the army were destroyed, leaving the civilian population entirely without sustenance or shelter for the winter.

As Sherman approached Savannah, he requested that troops in Beaufort move forward to cut the Charleston and Savannah Railroad. On November 28, a force of five thousand Union soldiers sailed from Hilton Head up the Broad River and discharged from their transports near Pocotaligo. Word of the threat was spread to Confederate authorities at both Charleston and Savannah, and forces were mustered from around the area. The primary contingent in the path of the Union force was the Third South Carolina Cavalry commanded by Colonel Charles J. Colcock, the same officer who went with Captain John Mickler on the reconnaissance of Pinckney Island raid in 1862. Under his superb and skillful leadership, the Yankees were delayed long enough for sufficient reinforcements to arrive and man an earthwork position, ordered erected by Robert E. Lee in 1861 at Honey Hill. There, the hastily assembled Confederates, including Georgia militia, soundly trounced the Union forces, inflicting almost eight hundred casualties while suffering fewer than fifty of their own. The Beaufort Volunteer Artillery contributed significantly to the victory with a pair of guns commanded by Captain Henry Stuart. The Yankees began withdrawing late that afternoon and returned to Hilton Head in great frustration.

Confederate forces holding Savannah were greatly outnumbered but held firm for ten days while Sherman prepared his army for an assault. On December 20, however, they evacuated the city when it was apparent that any defense would be futile and crossed the Savannah River into South Carolina, foiling Sherman's plans to trap them. The Yankees entered Savannah unopposed on December 21.

DECEMBER 9 FOUND GENERAL Beauregard and Stephen Elliott together once again. Beauregard, in command of Confederate forces in Savannah and South Carolina, sent a dispatch to the War Department in Richmond advising that "Brigadier-General Elliott, being temporarily in the department, has been assigned to command Third-Sub-District of South Carolina during the present emergency."[194] Despite his debilitating wounds and paralyzed arm, Elliott mustered sufficient strength to return for field duty, at least on a limited basis. Why he returned to active duty status while he was under a medical certificate excusing him for another month is not known. Perhaps it was Elliott's perception of responding to his ever-present sense of "doing his duty." He could have justifiably remained sidelined with his unhealed wounds without incurring a shred of criticism from any source. Fortunately, his area of responsibility was on the outskirts of Charleston at James Island and consisted mostly of observing enemy ship movements and activities in waters around some of the offshore islands. His new brigade command consisted of an assortment of artillery commands, including portions of the Twenty-Second and Twenty-Seventh Georgia Battalions, the Second South Carolina Artillery and Manigault's (S.C.) Battalion.

Sherman and his army celebrated the simultaneous joys of taking Savannah and Christmas festivities in a restrained manner, with few depredations or barbarous acts of terror inflicted on the gentle citizens in and around the city. As the Union army rested and resupplied, South Carolina correctly guessed that the Palmetto State would soon be Sherman's next target.

In late January 1865, Sherman began movement of his army with plans calling for him to pass through both Carolinas and join with Grant to defeat Lee in Virginia. General Beauregard and other Confederate commanders were unsure of the path he would take and could only make contingency plans. Charleston and Augusta, Georgia, were considered primary targets of his campaign, but with so few troops at their disposal, it was an impossible task to devise a workable plan of action until Sherman's plans were finally determined. Sherman set out, sending troops feinting toward both Charleston and Augusta but with the intent of marching to Columbia. The march was contested early on in a small action at the Battle of Rivers Bridge on February 3, in which a small Confederate force fought valiantly before being flanked and forced to withdraw. Sherman's cavalry meanwhile burned and pillaged along the South Carolina side of the Savannah River while advancing toward Augusta. Things were indeed looking bleak to Confederate commanders.

On February 10, Elliott was alerted by pickets that Union transports, supported by a monitor and several gunboats, were discharging troops on James Island. With an estimate of five thousand Yankees nearby, Elliott immediately called for one thousand reinforcements. That evening, he reported that his outer pickets had been driven in and the enemy was advancing. Fortunately, they stopped well before any threat to his position developed, but the situation remained tense over the next few days.[195]

Then, on February 15, Elliott received a lengthy dispatch of major importance. It opened with, "It has been determined to evacuate Charleston." This news, while shocking, was likely not unexpected in light of the threat of Sherman's army and other recent movements by the enemy around Charleston. The dispatch provides confirmation that Elliott was still suffering badly from the wounds received at Petersburg and expressed concerns about his health: "I have to beg that you will continue in command of the troops now with you, if you cannot longer, at least until you cross the Santee."[196] The dispatch then gave orders to spike his guns, destroy their carriages and dump their powder in water. It also called for preparation of rations and provided marching orders, rendezvous points and an evacuation date just two days away.

February 17, 1865, was a terrible day for the state of South Carolina. Sherman's army entered Columbia unopposed. The city was sacked and burned that night. Confederate forces evacuated Charleston that same evening as Beauregard began the consolidation of available forces to meet Sherman in the field of battle. Stephen Elliott and his brigade left their positions to join the procession of troops marching away from the city they had defended so long and successfully. His brigade of artillerymen, now to fight as infantry as part of the division commanded by Brigadier General W.B. Taliaferro, was reinforced by the Battalion of State Cadets (The Citadel). The men marched to St. Stephen on the Santee River, and, once there, Elliott had to decide whether he would continue with the army or step aside. He had honored the request made of him to lead his troops to that point. With no further obligation expected of him, what he did next was to be entirely his decision.

Undoubtedly, Elliott understood that the next several weeks with the army would be physically demanding. Long marches, exposure to the winter elements and encounters with the enemy were expected. There would be little rest and meager rations. All in all, his frail body would be taxed to the utmost if he stayed. The option of leaving it because of his physical frailties was certainly viable and anticipated by his superiors. Had he left the army, no blame or criticism could possibly be affixed to his name, nor would his reputation and honor be adversely affected. Elliott never explained his reasoning but apparently felt sufficiently strong enough to endure the anticipated difficulties. By staying with it, he was adhering to his strong personal sense of duty. His superior officers were likely pleasantly surprised on learning that he chose to remain with the army.

After a wait of several days, trains took the troops to Cheraw, South Carolina, where they made arrangements to continue the long march. With Sherman's army quickly approaching, Confederate forces began moving northward, still awaiting additional commands to arrive and bolster their strength. Elliott's Brigade was designated part of the army's rear guard and actually took occasional artillery fire from advanced Union commands as it marched forward. Elliott was so impressed by The Citadel cadets that he said, "When the danger is in the front, I put the Cadets in front and when the danger is in the rear, I put the Cadets in the rear."[197]

The march was tedious, and heavy rains flooded streams and rivers while at the same time turning roads into mud. General Elliott showed great courage and set a shining example to his troops by maintaining his post in such a physically demanding effort. Besides the rain and constant wetness, winter cold was a severe annoyance; this combination of nature's elements was sufficient to tax the strength of everyone. On March 10, just before the brigade reached Raleigh, North Carolina, the governor of South Carolina recalled the cadets with orders to rendezvous with him in Spartanburg, leaving Elliott with no unit with infantry experience.[198]

CONFEDERATE FORCES IN SOUTH Carolina had a change in command on February 22. General Joseph Johnston replaced Beauregard, who remained as Johnston's second in command. The army continued to retire in front of Sherman's forces, with constant cavalry engagements occurring around it. On March 15, Taliaferro's division was ordered to take a stand at Averasboro to test the strength of the advancing Yankees. A full battle was not expected nor wanted. Elliott's Brigade was positioned behind the front-line troops, who were expected to fall back and align with him if necessary. Artillery support of three guns, one of which was from the Beaufort Volunteer Artillery, was provided.

General Taliaferro's highly detailed after-action report dated April 4 reflects unusual courage and cohesion from the troops he commanded in the thirteen-hour engagement that followed. Beginning at 7:00 in the morning of March 16, the Yankees began shelling and assaulting the Confederate outer line, with the engagement reaching a crescendo at 11:00. Troops in the front line were finally forced to withdraw and take new positions around Elliott's Brigade. Over the next several hours, the Yankees made several demonstrations before making a flanking movement, causing a withdrawal to the main line of defense. A series of Union assaults soon followed, but each was thrown back. Union artillery regularly unleashed its fire on the Confederate position but failed to dislodge Taliaferro's men. Skirmishing lasted until 8:00 that evening. Shortly afterward, the division withdrew to rejoin the main force.

Taliaferro was justifiably proud of what his division had done that day in the face of intense fire. Greatly outnumbered, the hodgepodge collection of artillerymen with their muskets stood toe-to-toe against their blue-coated foe despite being greatly outnumbered. Taliaferro rightfully praised a number of officers and men who had performed well, starting his list with Stephen Elliott. The artillerymen-turned-infantry showed their grit and willingness to fight in an impressive manner, and Taliaferro gave them well-deserved recognition in his report. "The officers and men of my command, though unaccustomed to field fighting, behaved as well as troops could have done.

The discipline of garrison service, regular organization, and the daily exposure for eighteen months to the enemy's fire told in the coolness and determination with which they received the fire of the enemy."[199]

Casualties were high on each side. Of the twelve thousand Yankees involved that day, about seven hundred men were killed, wounded or missing. The Confederates lost nearly five hundred of their sixty-five hundred on the field.[200] The engagement showed that Johnston's army was still capable of putting up a fight.

Three days later, with nearly all of his army finally united, General Johnston saw an opportunity to halt his retreat and deploy his forces against the enemy. With Sherman's army advancing in two wings separated about a dozen miles apart, he sought to attack and smash Sherman's right wing at Bentonville, North Carolina, before Sherman's left wing could come to its assistance. It was a bold plan and one he hoped would catch Union commanders off guard and vulnerable. In the three-day battle that followed, Johnston's initial success was stopped by the superior numbers of his foe.

The battle commenced about 3:00 in the afternoon of March 19, and the unexpected Confederate assaults brushed away Union skirmishers and leading regiments. Stephen Elliott, on Johnston's right wing, led his troops forward, driving the retreating Yankees to their front. All along the line of attack, Confederate forces achieved initial success as they surged forward. However, Elliott's Brigade was stopped cold by heavy musketry along with accurate and deadly artillery fire as it exited a wood line into an open field. Suffering heavy casualties, it fell back to the woods, where a new line was formed.

Elsewhere, Union forces reacted quickly, eventually bringing the attack to a halt all across the field of battle. Massing their artillery and carrying out counterattacks, the Yankees succeeded in bringing order of chaos and drove the Confederates back. Elliott's Brigade remained in place along its new line and could only watch the fighting elsewhere on the field. The general remained with his battered command as it continued to be subjected to intense artillery fire, shattering limbs and branches of the trees around them. Taliaferro ordered Elliott's Brigade to lower their colors, have the men lie down and the officers kneel, in hopes the Yankee shelling would cease. Late that night, Taliaferro's division fell back to its original position. A conversation the next day between Elliott and a young courier on Taliaferro's staff whom Elliott knew is telling. Private Sam Ravenel, whose mother had been a close childhood friend of Elliott's, happened to be riding with the general, who asked him how he had felt facing the Union artillery the day before. Ravenel replied: "Why, General, I just felt that if I was going to be killed, all the trees could not save me; and if I was not, there was no need of one. The general gave that quiet laugh that all knew so well and, tapping me on my shoulder, said: 'My boy, as long as you are a soldier, that is the best belief in the world.'"[201]

General Johnston made no more assaults but left his army in position for two more days, hoping Sherman would attack. For the most part, those days were filled with skirmishing and shelling. On March 21, a Union assault threatening Johnston's route of retreat was blunted, and that night, Johnston gave orders for the army to withdraw from Bentonville. Though a Union victory, Johnston showed that his army was still a highly effective and capable fighting command. Casualty lists from both armies are incomplete, but best estimates show about sixteen hundred Yankees and twenty-five hundred Confederates were killed, wounded or missing after the engagement. One of the wounded Confederates was General Stephen Elliott, who suffered a painful leg wound. The wound was severe enough for him to relinquish command of his brigade and seek medical attention.[202] The general was likely unaware that his brother William, in the battle as a member of General Stephen Dill Lee's staff, was also wounded.

## 10

# THE GUNS GO SILENT
# (MAY 1865–FEBRUARY 1866)

April 1865 marked the end to the War Between the States. On April 2, Robert E. Lee's lines were broken at Petersburg, forcing him to evacuate Richmond and retreat westward across Virginia, with hopes of eventually linking up with Johnston's army. However, Union forces trapped him at Appomattox Court House a week later. On April 9, Lee surrendered his shattered, but still proud, Army of Northern Virginia. A few days later, Abraham Lincoln was assassinated. Joseph Johnston, still retreating toward Virginia with Sherman closely behind, declined to continue fighting after learning of Lee's surrender, viewing further military operations as a waste of life with an unobtainable goal. By surrendering his army to Sherman at Durham Station, North Carolina, on April 26, the goal of Southern independence was effectively ended. With Johnston's surrender, the men and officers of the army were paroled and allowed to return home. Stephen Elliott, with the army until the bitter end, was included in the paroles and went to Camden to rejoin his family.

Elliott returned to Beaufort in May for the first time since late 1861. The visit probably was emotionally draining, seeing the city filled with large numbers of Union troops, Freedmen's Bureau operatives and Northern carpetbaggers but only a handful of his family and friends. His land and property had been seized under the Confiscation Act of 1862, a law passed by the U.S. Congress allowing authorities to target Confederate military officers and public officeholders in the South by taking and disposing of their property while emancipating their slaves, if any. This same law was intended to quell opposition to Lincoln's governmental policies in the North as well, by subjecting Southern sympathizers to charges of treason punishable by huge fines, prison terms and even execution. Elliott was, in effect, homeless in May 1865. The land that had been his—and before that had belonged to his forefathers—now was in the hands of others.

ELLIOTT COMPLETED HIS VISIT and returned to Camden in June. There, he related an account of his Beaufort visit to Mary Boykin Chesnut, who recorded a portion of it in her diary.

> *He gave us an account of his father's plantation at Beaufort, from which he had just returned. "Our Negroes are living in great comfort. They were delighted to see me, and treated me with overflowing affection. They waited on me as before, gave me beautiful breakfasts and splendid dinners; but they firmly and respectfully informed me: 'we own this land now. Put it out of your head that it will ever be yours again.'"*[203]

Further complicating his circumstances was President Andrew Johnson's "Proclamation of Amnesty and Reconstruction" of May 29, 1865. In it, most Confederates were pardoned with citizenship and property rights restored provided they took the Oath of Allegiance to the United States. Fourteen classes of exceptions were excluded, however, and one of those was Confederate army officers having rank above lieutenant colonel. The proclamation required the excluded classes to submit a petition for restoration of citizenship and property rights directly to President Johnson.

Having had the rank of brigadier general in the Confederate army, Stephen Elliott was now also without citizenship and an opportunity to regain his lands unless he received Johnson's pardon. In late May, Mary Boykin Chesnut recorded in her diary that "Fighting Dick Anderson, and Stephen Elliott of Fort Sumter memory are quite ready to pray for Andy Johnson, and to submit to the powers that be."[204] Elliott saw, with the war concluded, that his personal duties and responsibilities were now to recover and rebuild for the benefit of his wife and two sons. Accordingly, on June 14, he penned a letter to President Johnson requesting restoration of citizenship and property rights while promising, "I intend to bear the U.S. Government the hearty allegiance which is due from every good citizen." The letter was forwarded to Elliott's former nemesis, Major General Quincy Gillmore, now back in Hilton Head as commanding officer of the Department of the South. Gillmore added his endorsement on June 16: "Respectfully forwarded. I believe Mr. Elliott's statement to be true in all respects."[205] The letter was received by the U.S. Attorney General in Washington and simply filed away on June 27 with no action taken.[206]

On August 3, he took the Oath of Allegiance to the United States and, two days later, submitted another letter to Johnson petitioning for restoration of citizenship and property rights. The letter and oath were forwarded together by the Union officer administering the oath, who endorsed the application: "Approved and respectfully forwarded. It may be added that General Elliott has the reputation of having been very kind to all prisoners whom he captured." The documents were received and again filed by the U.S. Attorney General in Washington on August 31 with no action taken.[207]

Sometime afterward, Stephen Elliott moved his family from Camden to the Beaufort area with hopes of recovering at least some of his land. There, he took up residence in a small fishing shack on the beach, within sight of his old home, which he had built many years before. To provide for his family, Elliott returned to one of the passions of his early days: fishing. His skills in that pursuit were sufficiently productive to provide at least a meager subsistence for his family by selling his catches around the Port Royal area. With only one good arm, his efforts must have been physically exacting and difficult.[208]

In late October, having heard nothing about his pardon, Stephen Elliott took another step toward obtaining the pardon so desperately needed. He called directly on General Gillmore at his headquarters on Hilton Head Island. The decision to approach Gillmore was likely difficult to make, but tough times call for tough decisions, and Elliott went forward. There is no record of their conversation, but these two men who had been such ardent foes for eight months came face to face in a setting far different than when they had opposed each other. Elliott explained his circumstances to Gillmore and asked his assistance in obtaining the pardon from President Johnson. Gillmore must have marveled at meeting the man who had defied his efforts to bombard Fort Sumter into submission with unbridled courage, audacity and perseverance but now was impoverished. Whatever his thoughts and emotions might have been, he was won over to Elliott's cause, for on October 25, he wrote a letter directly to Johnson, urging the president to grant a pardon for Elliott. His personal evaluation of Elliott probably swayed the president into action. "I know of no more worthy object of Executive Clemency, among the officers lately arrayed against the Union, than himself. He is a high toned gentleman, & a man of faith and probity, and I earnestly recommend his case for early consideration." President Johnson acted quickly after receiving Gillmore's letter and, on November 4, authorized Executive Clemency for Stephen Elliott.[209]

ELLIOTT HAD TAKEN OTHER steps toward recovery from his circumstances by offering himself as a candidate for the state House of Representatives and winning election. His name was still strong in Beaufort, and even those from "up-north" supported him. Assigned to the Military Committee and Federal Relations Committee, he was sworn into the legislature on November 3.[210] Just a few days later, he announced that he would run as a candidate for the U.S. Congress. His plans and hopes were high even in these dark times.[211] With his pardon, Stephen Elliott now had all the rights and privileges of U.S. citizenship. However, he was unable to regain rights to his property, some of which had been sold and the balance retained by the Freedmen's Bureau.[212]

In early 1866, another promising avenue of recovery came to him when he was appointed to a position on the South Carolina Railroad.[213] Unfortunately, right behind this good piece of news, his health took a turn for the worse. While in Aiken for business, Elliott fell ill. His condition gradually deteriorated, and on February 21, the general passed away. In a conversation with his father near the end, Elliott comforted him: "I am safe in Jesus." His last request was to be buried by his mother in Beaufort.[214] His death was attributed to the wounds received at The Crater and the harsh demands made on his body afterward.

Elliott's death rang across the state of South Carolina and far beyond its borders. It was chronicled in numerous Northern newspapers in various forms, ranging from simple announcements to full-scale obituary columns reserved for those of prominence. The Philadelphia *Evening Telegraph* article announcing his death called him "The Rebel Hero of Fort Sumter" in its headline. One paragraph referred to his reputation and high standing with General Gillmore.

> *Elliott was placed in command of Fort Sumter, and continued to command its defenses during the terrible bombardment to which it was subjected by General Gillmore. Gillmore is said to have admired the defense of Elliott very highly, and to have so far shown his regard for the soldierly*

*qualities displayed by him as to take steps to secure his early pardon by the President.*[215]

The obituary provided a detailed account of Elliott's life in a lengthy column. Further, it described his funeral in a manner leaving no doubt that Stephen Elliott Jr. had an elaborate funeral, one worthy of a legend and hero.

*Requiescat in pace*

# EPILOGUE

Stephen Elliott Jr. left behind a grieving widow with two young sons and a legacy reflecting the worthy qualities of a loving husband, a fine soldier, a man of faith and one who held himself to the highest standards in performing his duties in all that he did regardless of circumstances. He gained respect and confidence of those he served under or commanded in the war by leading by example. Whether it was in small raids, during the bombardments at Fort Sumter or on the battlefields of Petersburg and North Carolina, Stephen Elliott was there with his men, sharing the same dangers and difficulties they did. His superior officers respected him not only as a man, but also as a highly capable officer in whom they could safely place their trust and confidence. He must have possessed the rare trait of "command presence," one that instantly reflected a steady nerve and self-confidence in a manner calming to all those with whom he came in contact.

Elliott never once resorted to political posturing for promotion or recognition. His superb service spoke for itself. Special attention given him by Beauregard, Lee and President Jefferson Davis was well earned and deserving. His service was "at the front," and as such he was wounded in five separate engagements with the enemy. His ability to inspire those serving in his command is reflected by the special courage exhibited in numerous actions of the Beaufort Volunteer Artillery, the troops at Fort Sumter and those he later led at Petersburg and in the Carolinas Campaign.

The South Carolina State House of Representatives recognized him during the September 1866 session with a lengthy eulogy so profound that

# Epilogue

one thousand copies of it were published in pamphlet form for distribution.[216] His name and reputation remained vivid throughout South Carolina long after his death. When former Confederate soldiers established the United Confederate Veterans in the early 1890s, South Carolina's very first camp, in St. George, adopted the name of the "Stephen Elliott" UCV Camp no. 51.[217] In 1910, the Stephen Elliott Chapter no. 1349, United Daughters of the Confederacy, was formed and continues its good work through today.

THE ELLIOTT FAMILY PATRIARCH, Reverend Stephen Elliott Sr., died on March 13, just a few short weeks after laying his son to rest. His obituary stated, "He died in Beaufort…of a disease contracted while in attendance of the obsequies of his beloved son." It noted that the loss of two sons in his later years weighed heavily on him.[218]

Charlotte Elliott joined her beloved husband in death on April 23, 1868, in Beaufort.[219] The storybook life and future that had been so promising for the young couple ended much too soon for each of them. She was just thirty-five years of age and left the couple's two young sons to be cared for by relatives. Their son Henry Stuart Elliott (1858–1942) traveled westward and lived in Wyoming, where he married. Later, he and his family moved to Washington State, where he had distinguished service as a judge. Their other son, Charles Pinckney Elliott (1860–1943), graduated from West Point and served in the U.S. Army before being retired in 1898 under a disability following service in the Spanish-American War. He was returned to active duty in World War 1 but did not go to Europe. His most well-remembered military service was when, as a young lieutenant, he campaigned against the famed American Indian chief Geronimo. Charles died in Beaufort while on a fishing trip.

Stephen Elliott's brother William (1839–1907) survived the war and is said to have been promoted to lieutenant colonel in the last months of the struggle. Returning to Beaufort, he made a name for himself as an attorney and, as a Democrat, served several terms as a U.S. congressman between 1887 and 1903. President Teddy Roosevelt appointed him commissioner in charge of marking Confederate graves in cemeteries at or near former U.S. prisoner-of-war camps in the north. The first markers obtained went to Elmira, New York, and the next set was sent to Camp Chase, Ohio. Though he died suddenly in 1907 after just a year into his work, William's efforts set the standard for completion of this vital project, which continued under others following his guidelines and examples.

# Epilogue

Middleton Stuart Elliott (1841–1921) excelled in his experience as a private in the engineering department and obtained a commission as a second lieutenant in the Engineering Corps in April 1864. His obituary stated that he was present during the fighting at The Crater and received a slight head wound in the affair. After the war, he returned to Beaufort, married and raised his family there. At one time he was in business with his brother-in-law Henry Stuart.

Young Henry D. Elliott (1848–1907) returned to Beaufort from the war and successfully lived his life there. He fathered several children and named two of his sons Stephen and Ralph.

John H. Elliott (1832–1906) remained an Episcopal clergyman and spent much of his life in Washington, D.C., where he died. His brother William, who served many years in Washington as a congressman and likely spent much time with John, brought his body to Beaufort for burial.

One young man not mentioned elsewhere in this work is Stephen Elliott Barnwell (1842–1923), a prewar neighbor of Stephen Elliott Jr. For some reason, despite the age difference, Elliott and Barnwell developed a close friendship, and Barnwell served with Elliott during most of the war. Enlisting in the Beaufort Volunteer Artillery, Barnwell performed well enough to be promoted to sergeant and sought commission as an officer on at least two occasions. In September 1863, after being posted to Fort Sumter, Elliott formally requested Barnwell be detached to the Torpedo Branch in Charleston and, shortly afterward, requested his services at Fort Sumter. By accepting detachment to Sumter, Barnwell lost his sergeant's stripes and reverted to private. Family records state he served as Elliott's acting adjutant at Sumter even though he was a private. When Elliott took command of the Holcombe Legion, the adjutant billet was vacant. He immediately requested Barnwell be appointed as its adjutant, and the request was authorized, resulting in Barnwell's promotion to lieutenant. Upon Elliott's promotion to brigadier general, he promptly requested Barnwell be appointed his volunteer aide-de-camp, a request that was also approved. The position of aide-de-camp (ADC) was the only one a general could place on his personal staff at his discretion and was usually reserved for someone whom the general trusted fully and knew closely.[220] It is for these reasons that Barnwell is mentioned in this section. Barnwell served with Elliott in Virginia and Charleston and during the Carolinas Campaign and, like Elliott, was wounded at Bentonville. No other man served so much time with Elliott during the war as did young Barnwell.

# Epilogue

General William S. Walker was exchanged on October 29, 1864, and soon returned to active duty in an administrative position in North Carolina, where he served until the war's end. Afterward, he moved to Georgia and died in Atlanta in 1899. He, like Stephen Elliott, was a superb choice as brigade commander. Favored by both Robert E. Lee and P.G.T. Beauregard, Walker was recognized as an excellent officer.

Captain Thomas Champneys never returned to Fort Sumter. His engineering skills and personal courage so evident at Battery Wagner and Fort Sumter were clearly acknowledged by those with whom he served. He and Stephen Elliott formed a dynamic duo in returning Fort Sumter to more than an isolated picket post.

Captain John Johnson, another engineer, served under Captain Champneys at both Battery Wagner and Fort Sumter. He succeeded Champneys at Sumter and worked closely with Stephen Elliott. His diligence, energy and imagination never wavered, and he was certainly a positive influence at the fort. Johnson remained a driving force in the continued recovery at Sumter until he was badly wounded and crippled in late 1864. A native Charlestonian, he became an active and leading citizen in the city after the war. His book *The Defense of Charleston Harbor Including Fort Sumter and the Adjacent Islands 1863–1865* is considered one of the finest and most authoritative accounts of the war around Charleston.

Union general Quincy Gillmore's service in Virginia was short-lived. He performed fairly well at times in the Bermuda Hundred Campaign but

Fort Sumter's appearance in an 1865 Union photograph. *Library of Congress.*

# Epilogue

showed little genius in leading a field command. He failed completely in the First Battle of Petersburg and, after a bitter feud with his commanding officer, General Benjamin Butler, was relieved and sent to serve in administrative posts for the duration of the war. At its end, he returned to Hilton Head in command of the Department of the South, a post he held until resigning from the army in December 1865. He successfully returned to the field of engineering and, after his wife died, married the widow of Confederate general Braxton Bragg.

Fort Sumter remained in Confederate hands until Charleston was evacuated in February 1865. Union guns on Morris Island continued their shelling, but the fort's commanding officers and engineers continued the exceptional work started by Stephen Elliott and his stalwart engineers, Captains Champneys and Johnson. When evacuated, living quarters were greatly expanded, debris was removed and the fort was at its strongest.

The image on the book cover is of an india ink sketch of a photograph taken by famed photographer George S. Cook at Fort Sumter on December 9, 1863. This sketch, by a skilled artist, was commissioned by General P.G.T. Beauregard and presented to Stephen Elliott in April 1864 as a formal presentation piece in the same manner as a presentation sword or firearm. Intended to show Beauregard's appreciation to Elliott for superb service, the inscription on the original reads, "To Lt. Col. Step. Elliott, P.A.C.S. Artillery, Cmdg. Fort Sumter, With Compliments of General Beauregard." Additional notes show the sketch was given by Elliott to Union general Quincy Gillmore in late 1865, almost certainly in appreciation for Gillmore's effort to assist Elliott in regaining citizenship. Elliott would have had few personal treasures at the time, and it probably pained him to part with this. This unique story confirms a friendly and respectful postwar relationship between the two men.

# APPENDIX A

The December 6, 1863 letter from General J.F. Gilmer, Beauregard's senior subordinate in Charleston, requesting additional rank for Lieutenant Colonel Stephen Elliott is shown verbatim. Gilmer's reasons justifying this request, just a week after Elliott was promoted to lieutenant colonel, reflect the respect and esteem held for Elliott throughout the military organization in Charleston. Though it did not result in an immediate promotion, the letter likely had great influence in his promotion from lieutenant colonel of artillery to colonel of infantry five months later under different circumstances.

Headquarters
Department of South Carolina, Ga. & Fla.
Atlanta, Ga. Dec.6th, 1863

Hon. J.A. Seddon
Secretary of War

Sir,
Just now leaving Charleston for this place, I had an interview with Genl. Beauregard in which I took occasion to present the services of Major—now Lieut. Col.—Stephen Elliott commanding Fort Sumter since the 1$^{st}$ September last. His conduct since his assignment to the command has been such as to attract the attention, and receive approbation of all his superior officers, and to secure the full confidence and support of the

# Appendix A

whole garrison—men and officers—who have served under him. His energy, judgement, and coolness, under all circumstances, has been such as to call forth the admiration of all the brave troops now engaged in the defense of Charleston. Genl. Beauregard concurs fully in all I have said, and with his consent, and full endorsement, I respectfully request as a special mark of approbation that the government confer, at once, an additional grade upon Lt. Col. Elliott. The defense of "Sumter" as conducted by him, is one destined to be memorable in the history of our country, and I ask special notice of the commander, not only because it is well merited, but also because prompt action will encourage others in in our further efforts to stay the invader, and force him to abandon his attempts to lay in ruins the city of Charleston.

I am Sir, very respectfully your obdt.svnt.
J.F. Gilmer
Major Genl. & 2$^{nd}$ in Command

# APPENDIX B

Included in this Appendix are each of the two letters from Stephen Elliott Jr. to President Andrew Johnson requesting amnesty. Also included is the letter on Elliott's behalf from Major General Quincy Gillmore to President Johnson. They are taken verbatim from the Confederate Amnesty Papers held by the National Archives.[221]

Camden So. Car. June 14th, 1865

To His Excellency Andrew Johnson
President United States of America

Sir,
In pursuance of the clause for the exercise of Executive Clemency as put forth in the Amnesty Proclomation of May 29th, I respectfully beg that the rights of citizenship and property be extended to my case.

I entered service as a Capt and have been promoted until I reached in May 1864 the rank of Brigadier. My service has been chiefly on the coast of SC but I also served in Virginia and was attached when paroled with General Johnston's army. I have always carried out in strict conformity with civilized customs and invariably treated prisoners with kindness as can be substantiated by the testimony of U.S. officers.

I am a native of South Carolina and owned property near Port Royal. This property so far as I can see has not been sold.

# Appendix B

I intend to bear the U.S. government the hearty allegiance which is due from every good citizen and I honestly beg that I may be admitted to the rights of citizenship and property under such regulations as may be adopted by the authorities.
I am Sir,
Very respectfully your obsert,
Stephen Elliott, Jr.
Brig Genl Late C.S.A.

Camden S.C.
August 5$^{th}$, 1865

To His Excellency Andrew Johnson
President of the United States

Sir,
I have the honor respectfully to submit this petition praying to be admitted to the privileges of the amnesty Proclamation.

Commencing the war as a Captain I served in successive grades upon the coast of South Carolina and more especially at Charleston until April 1864 when I was ordered to Virginia and made a Brigadier. At Petersburg I received a wound which has deprived me of the use of an arm. When paroled, I was attached to Genl Johnston's army.

This application is made in good faith and I propose henceforward to bear full and true allegiance to the United States Government.
Very Respectfully,
Your obt servant,
Stephen Elliott, Jr.

Hd Quarters Dept of South Carolina
Hilton Head SC

To The President of the United States
Washington, D.C.

I most respectfully urge, if there exist no special reasons to the contrary, that the application for pardon of Mr. Stephen Elliott, late a Brigadier General in the rebel army, receive early attention.

# Appendix B

Mr. Elliott is now residing in this vicinity, supports himself and family as best he can, by fishing. He was, at the beginning of the war, the owner of considerable land in the neighborhood of Port Royal, which is now in the custody of agents of the Freedmen's Bureau, and he would probably soon be restored to the possession of some of it, were he to received pardon. I know of no more worthy object of Executive Clemency, among the officers lately arrayed against the Union, than himself.

He is a high toned gentleman, & a man of faith and probity, and I earnestly recommend his case for early consideration.

Very Respectfully,
Your obnt Servant,
Q.A. Gillmore, Maj. Genl

# NOTES

## Chapter 1

1. Edgar, *South Carolina*, 293–94.
2. *1860 U.S. Federal Census*. Slave Schedule of that year shows that Stephen Elliott Jr. owned 49 slaves of which 26 were males and 23 females. Fifteen of them were children under 10 years of age. Ten were aged 40 to over 60 and the rest were between 10 and 39.
3. *Compiled Service Records of Confederate Soldiers Who Served in Organizations from the State of South Carolina*, Roll 0248. Letter of November 2, 1862, from General Walker states Elliott was captain of the BVA for four years prior to the outbreak of war.
4. "South Carolina Legislature," *Southern Enterprise*, November 15, 1860, 2.
5. Elliott Family Papers, South Caroliniana Library, University of South Carolina, Columbia, SC. Letter from General W.S. Walker, dated November 15, 1862.
6. Elliott Family Papers.

## Chapter 2

7. *Compiled Service Records*, Rolls 0155 & 0248; *1860 U.S. Federal Census*; Baker, *Cadets in Gray*, 39.
8. Baxley, *No Prouder Fate*, 4–5.

9. *Mercury*, May 21, 1861, 2, and July 16, 1861, 2; "In the Court of the Confederate States–District of South Carolina," August 3, 1861, 4; "News of the Day," *New York Times*, August 29, 1861; *Official Records of the Union and Confederate Navies*, 30 volumes, Washington, D.C., U.S. Government Printing Office, 1894–1922), series 1, vol. 5, 649–58. Hereafter cited as *OR Navies*.
10. *War of the Rebellion: A Compilation of the Official Records of Union and Confederate Armies*, series 1, vol. 6, 6. Hereafter cited as *OR* and, unless otherwise noted, taken from series 1.
11. *OR*, 1, vol. 53, 73. Emphasis added.
12. Baxley, *No Prouder Fate*, 23; *OR* 1, vol. 6, 11–12, 26; "Death of Rev. Stephen Elliott," *Intelligencer*, March 22, 1866, 1.
13. *OR*, vol. 6, 28; *Compiled Service Records*, Roll 0248.
14. *OR*, vol. 6, 28.
15. Ibid.
16. *OR*, vol. 6, 1; *Observer*, November 13, 1861; "Camp Notes," *Enquirer*, December 5, 1861, 2.
17. *OR*, vol. 6, 26.
18. Ibid., 11.
19. "Since Taking the Forts," *Enquirer*, December 5, 1861, 2.
20. Ibid., 34.
21. "The War on the Coast," *Mercury*, December 9, 1861, 2.
22. Elliott Family Papers.

## Chapter 3

23. *OR*, vol. 6, 1.
24. *Compiled Service Records*, Roll 0085.
25. *OR*, vol. 14, 20–27.
26. Ibid., 24.
27. Ibid., 26.
28. "The Beaufort Artillery," *Mercury*, June 9, 1862, 2.
29. *OR*, vol.14, 31–32.
30. Baker, *Cadets in Gray*, 67; *Compiled Service Records*, Roll 0248.
31. *OR*, vol.14, 112.
32. Ibid., 117–18.
33. Ibid., 118–19.
34. Ibid., 115–17, 119; "The Night Attack on The Yankee Camp on Pinckney Island," *Mercury*, August 28, 1862, 1.

35. *OR.*, vol. 14, 118.
36. Ibid., 119. Captain Mickler performed many daring scouts during the course of the war. His brothers, William and Huger, served as scouts in Virginia. William was first commander of General Wade Hampton's famed "Iron Scouts," and Huger served in that esteemed detachment until his death in April 1863.
37. "Obituaries," *Mercury*, September 9, 1862, 2.
38. *OR*, vol.14, 632–33.
39. Ibid., 144–46.
40. Ibid., 180–81.
41. Ibid., 181–82; Capers, *Confederate Military History*, vol. 5, *South Carolina*, 102–5.
42. *OR*, vol. 14, 180, 148, 184–87.
43. Ibid., 151.
44. Ibid., 183. An excellent account of the fighting that day at Pocotaligo and Coosawhatchie is found in Baxley's *No Prouder Fate*, 57–65.
45. Roman, *The Military Operations of General Beauregard*. vol. 2, 33; *Compiled Service Records*, Roll 0085.
46. Hudson, *Sketches and Reminiscences*, 37.
47. *Compiled Service Records*, Roll 0105.
48. *Compiled Service Records*, Roll 0109. Service records for Reverend Elliott and his son Stephen Jr. are found inexplicably placed together in a single record under the name "Stephen Elliott" under "Officers."
49. "Army Gossip from the Coast," *Mercury*, December 16, 1862, 2.

## Chapter 4

50. *Compiled Service Records*, Roll 0105. Emphasis added.
51. Ibid. Emphasis added.
52. *OR*, vol. 14, 280–84; "The Situation," *News*, April 29, 1863, 1.
53. *Compiled Service Records*, Roll 0105; *OR*, vol. 28, pt. 2, 271–72, 292.
54. *Compiled Service Records*, Roll 0085.
55. Ibid., Roll 0105.
56. Underwood and Buel, *Battles and Leaders*, vol. 4, 54–55.
57. Ibid., 60.
58. Ibid., 60–62; *OR*, vol. 28, pt. 1, 648–650.
59. Underwood and Buel, *Battles and Leaders*, vol. 4, 62; Barnes, *Fort Sumter*, 28.

60. Underwood and Buel, *Battles and Leaders*, vol. 4, 72–74; Wilcox and Ripley, *Civil War at Charleston*, 55.
61. Underwood and Buel, *Battles and Leaders*, vol. 4, 66, 72–74; Barnes, *Fort Sumter*, 30.
62. "The Siege," *Mercury*, October 7, 1863, 2.
63. *OR*, vol. 28, pt. 1, 651.
64. Ibid., 653–54.
65. Underwood and Buel, *Battles and Leaders*, vol. 1, 83.
66. *OR*, vol. 28, pt. 1, 651, 654.
67. Underwood and Buel, *Battles and Leaders*, vol. 4, 18–19.
68. Roman, *Military Operations of General Beauregard*, 151–52. Emphasis added.
69. Ibid., 152; Johnson, *Defense of Charleston Harbor*, 155–56.
70. Johnson, *Defense of Charleston Harbor*, 155–156. Johnson wrote that Beauregard regarded Elliott highly with this statement about Elliott: "With his superior officers he stood well; and General Beauregard, from knowing him personally and hearing his good report for gallantry and self-reliance, sent for him."
71. Ibid., 148; *OR*, vol. 28, pt. 2, 309, 336.
72. Johnson, *Defense of Charleston Harbor*, 149.
73. Elliott Family Papers.

## *Chapter 5*

74. *OR*, vol. 28, pt. 1, 621–22.
75. John Johnson Papers. Documents included in this invaluable collection are Elliott's Order Book and Book of Letters covering the period he was in command at Fort Sumter.
76. *OR*, vol. 28, p.1, 622.
77. Johnson Papers.
78. *OR*, vol. 28, 120–25, 726–27; Elliott Family Papers, letter of September 8, 1863.
79. *OR*, vol. 28, pt. 1, 122–23.
80. *OR*, vol. 28, pt. 2, 344.
81. Johnson, *Defense of Charleston*, 155.
82. Elliott Family Papers. The "Cook, artist" Elliott referred to was famed southern photographer George S. Cook. He is renowned for taking the first combat action photograph in history on September 8, 1863, as Union ironclads exchanged gunfire with Fort Moultrie in the action as described

in Elliott's letter. He also captured the explosion of a Yankee shell in the interior of Fort Sumter in a photograph taken later in 1863.
83. Johnson, *Defense of Charleston*, 162–63.
84. Underwood and Buel, *Battles and Leaders*, vol. 4, 50.
85. *OR Navies*, vol. 14, 630.
86. *OR*, vol. 28, pt. 1, 727.
87. Ibid., 125, 403, 606, 724–28; Underwood and Buel, *Battles and Leaders*, vol. 4, 47–51, 65; see also *OR Navies*, vol. 14, 77, 80, 159–64, 607–36. These refences provide detailed and clear reports of the assault from both sides and especially so from a variety of Union participants. For such a comparatively small engagement, the number of sources is amazing.
88. *OR*, vol. 28, pt. 2, 349.
89. *OR*, vol. 28, pt. 1, 728.
90. Johnson, *Defense of Charleston Harbor*, 167.
91. "The Siege," *Mercury*, September 18, 1863, 2.
92. *Compiled Service Records*, Roll 0105.
93. *OR*, vol. 28, pt. 1, 132–33.
94. Ibid., 127.
95. Ibid., 129.
96. Ibid., 130.
97. Ibid., 131.
98. Ibid.
99. Johnson, *Defense of Charleston Harbor*, 169, Appendix, page xlv.
100. *OR*, vol. 28, pt. 1, 654–55.
101. Ibid., 134.
102. *OR*, vol. 28, pt. 2, 374–75.
103. Johnson Papers, Elliott's order book.
104. *OR*, vol. 28, pt. 1, 136. This affair seems to have had no effect on the captain's standing within his regiment according to the *Compiled Service Records*. In November 1863, just weeks after being dismissed from Fort Sumter, he was promoted to regimental major. In August 1864, after heavy fighting near Petersburg, he temporarily commanded the regiment.
105. *OR*, vol. 28, pt. 1, 136, 626.
106. Ibid., 648; Johnson, *Defense of Charleston Harbor*, 169.
107. *OR*, vol. 28, pt. 1, 138; Johnson, *Defense of Charleston Harbor*, 169.
108. *OR*, vol. 28, pt. 1, 140.
109. Johnson Papers.

110. Ibid.
111. *OR*, vol. 28, pt. 1, 145.
112. Johnson Papers; Johnson, *Defense of Charleston Harbor*, 170.
113. Underwood and Buel, *Battles and Leaders*, vol. 4, 26; Johnson, *Defense of Charleston Harbor*, 173–74; *OR*, vol. 28, pt. 1, 158.
114. Johnson, *Defense of Charleston Harbor*, 174; Underwood and Buel, *Battles and Leaders*, vol. 4, 26.
115. *OR*, vol. 28, pt. 1, 147.
116. Johnson Papers.
117. Underwood and Buel, *Battles and Leaders*, vol. 4, 66–67; Barnes, *Fort Sumter*, 33.
118. *OR*, vol. 28, pt. 1, 149–50, 649.
119. Ibid., 668–69, 649.
120. Ibid., 152.
121. Ibid; 152, 650; Johnson, *Defense of Charleston of Charleston Harbor*, 172.
122. *OR*, vol. 28, pt. 1, 649.
123. "The Siege-One Hundred and Twelfth Day," *Mercury*, October 31, 1863, 2. Emphasis added.
124. *OR*, vol. 28, pt. 1, 153.
125. Witt and Capers, "Flag of the Twelfth Georgia Artillery," 113.
126. *OR*, vol. 28, pt.1, 153; Ellington, *Confederate Flags*, 38–39.
127. *OR*, vol. 28, pt. 2, 466.
128. *OR*, vol. 28, pt. 1, 154.
129. *OR*, vol. 28, pt. 2, 487.
130. *OR*, vol. 28, pt. 1, 154; Johnson, *Defense of Charleston Harbor*, 174.
131. *OR*, vol. 28, pt. 2, 471, 474–75; *OR*, Vol. 28, pt. 1, 154–55.
132. *OR*, vol. 28, pt. 1, 155.
133. *OR*, vol. 28, pt. 2, 489; *Compiled Service Records*, Roll 0105.
134. *OR*, vol. 28, pt. 1, 167, 743.
135. Johnson, *Defense of Charleston Harbor*, 175; Barnes, *Fort Sumter*, 35.
136. *OR*, vol. 28, pt. 1, 605–06.
137. *OR*, vol. 28, pt. 1, 167–68, 743.
138. Ibid., 171; *OR*, vol. 28, pt. 2, 555; Underwood and Buel, *Battles and Leaders*, 25–26.
139. *OR*, vol. 28, pt. 1, 621, 635, 606.
140. Ibid., 649–50.
141. Chesnut, *Diary from Dixie*, 327.
142. *Compiled Service Records*, Roll 0105.
143. "Major Elliott Promoted," *Mercury*, December 1, 1863, 2.

144. Chesnut, *Diary from Dixie*, 327. Sandy Hill was a plantation near Camden, South Carolina, owned by the Chesnut family.
145. Underwood and Buel, *Battles and Leaders*, vol. 4, 65–66.
146. Ibid., 26.
147. *Compiled Service Records*, Roll 0085.
148. Ibid.
149. *OR*, vol. 28, pt. 1, 649; Johnson, *Defense of Charleston Harbor*, appendix, xv.
150. Underwood and Buel, *Battles and Leaders*, vol. 4, 25; *OR*, vol. 28, pt. 1, 177, 643–45; Johnson, *Defense of Charleston Harbor*, 189–95; Wilcox and Ripley, *Civil War at Charleston*, 69.
151. *OR*, vol. 28, pt. 1, 643–44.
152. Ibid., 645–46.
153. Elliott Family Papers.
154. *OR*, vol. 28, pt. 2, 555.
155. Johnson, *Defense of Charleston*, appendix, xv.
156. *OR*, vol. 28, pt. 1, 184–85; vol. 28, pt. 2, 580–81; Gene Sapakoff, "Charleston's Worst Christmas," *Post and Courier*, December 23, 2013.
157. Johnson, *Defense of Charleston Harbor*, 197–98.
158. *OR*, vol. 28, pt. 1, 189; *OR*, vol. 35, pt. 1, 176.

## Chapter 6

159. *OR*, vol. 35, pt. 1, 177–78.
160. Ibid., 180.
161. Johnson, *Defense of Charleston Harbor*, 198; *OR*, vol. 35, pt. 1, 181–83. Daily reports of January 21–27 are signed by Captain F.T. Miles.
162. *OR*, vol. 35, pt. 1, 181–82.
163. Ibid., 186.
164. Ibid., 184–85; Johnson, *Defense of Charleston Harbor*, 199.
165. *OR*, vol. 35, pt. 1, 192.
166. Johnson, *Defense of Charleston Harbor*, appendix, xvi.
167. "Siege Matters," *Mercury*, February 26, 1864, 2.
168. *OR*, vol. 35, pt. 1, 193.
169. Ibid., 201.
170. Ibid., 204, *Defense of Charleston Harbor*, appendix, xvi; Fort Sumter's daily reports April 15–25 were signed by Captain J.C. Mitchel. Elliott returned from furlough the evening of the twenty-fifth. Captain Mitchel succeeded Elliott as commander of Fort Sumter in May 1864.

## Chapter 7

171. Elliot Family Papers.
172. Ibid.
173. "Siege Matters," 1.
174. Elliott Family Papers.
175. Ibid.
176. *Compiled Service Records*, Roll 0085.
177. Elliott Family Papers.
178. Ibid.
179. Ibid.
180. *Compiled Service Records*, Roll 0155.
181. Elliott Family Papers.
182. "Death of Brigadier-General Elliott," *Enquirer*, March 8, 1866, 1. This obituary was a lengthy one detailing his full military service. Whether he was hit by spent balls or shrapnel at Petersburg is unknown. No mention of this is found elsewhere. Wounds from spent balls could still cause painful bruises. If he was hit by shrapnel, it was likely minor in nature, since no hospital records are found.
183. "Saturday's Operations near Petersburg," *Daily Dispatch*, June 20, 1864.

## Chapter 8

184. *OR*, vol. 40, pt. 1, 782–83, 775, 778 and 780.
185. *OR*, vol. 40, pt. 1, 787–88.
186. "Elliott's Brigade in the Crater Fight," *The State*, March 5, 1899.
187. *OR*, vol. 40, pt. 1, 790.
188. *Compiled Service Records*, Roll 0085.
189. Chesnut, *Diary From Dixie*, 426.
190. "Condition of General Elliott," *Mercury*, August 11, 1864, 2.
191. *Compiled Service Records*, Roll 0085.

## Chapter 9

192. Ibid.
193. "Siege Matters—Four Hundred and Ninety-Eighth Day," *Mercury*, November 19, 1864, 2.

194. *OR*, vol. 44, 942.
195. *OR*, vol. 47, pt. 2, 1142.
196. Ibid., 1195.
197. Baker, *Cadets in Gray*, 160–61.
198. Ibid.
199. *OR*, vol. 47, pt. 1, 1084–86; vol. 47, pt. 2, 1402.
200. *OR*, vol. 47, 66. Union reports totaled 682 men as casualties but some unit reports had yet to be submitted.
201. Samuel W. Ravenel, "The Boy Brigade of South Carolina," *Confederate Veteran* 29, 1921, 417.
202. Bradley, *Last Stand in the Carolinas*, 286; Trescot, *Late General Stephen Elliott*, 20; "Death of Brigadier-General Elliott," 1.

## Chapter 10

203. Chesnut, *Diary from Dixie*, 540.
204. Ibid., 536.
205. *Confederate Amnesty Papers, Case Files of Applications from Former Confederates for Presidential Pardons ("Amnesty Papers")*, National Archives, M653, South Carolina, Roll 1214.
206. Ibid.
207. Ibid.
208. Trescot, *Late General Stephen Elliott*, 21.
209. Ibid.
210. "Legislature South Carolina," *Daily Phoenix*, November 5, 1865; Hutson and Trescot, *In Memorium: Gen. Stephen Elliott*, 21.
211. "For Congress, General Stephen Elliott, Jr.," *Daily News*, November 9, 1865, 4.
212. *Confederate Amnesty Papers*.
213. "Death of Brigadier-General Stephen Elliott," 1; in December 1865, he is shown as one of the Hilton Head commissioners for the Deep Water and Western Railroad, a prospective new railroad, in an announcement seeking investors. See *Daily News*, December 30, 1865, 4.
214. *Extract from Journal of House of Representatives*, 8; Trescot, *Late General Stephen Elliott*, 22.
215. "The Rebel General Stephen Elliott, Jr., of South Carolina," *Evening Telegraph*, March 27, 1866, 7.

## Epilogue

216. *Extract from Journal of House of Representatives.*
217. "Well Done, Good and Faithful Servants," *Confederate Veteran*, no. 1, 1894, 269.
218. "Death of Rev. Stephen Elliott."
219. "Obituaries," *Daily News*, April 30, 1866.
220. Krick, *Staff Officers in Gray*, 374. Krick's detailed study of how ADCs were used, pages 10–14, is highly informative. Barnwell is listed among Elliott's staff on page 374.

## Appendix B

221. *Confederate Amnesty Papers.*

# BIBLIOGRAPHY

*Books and Articles*

Baker, Gary R. *Cadets in Gray: The Story of the Cadets of the South Carolina Military Academy and the Cadet Rangers in the Civil War.* Columbia, SC: Palmetto Bookworks, 1989.
Barnes, Frank. *Fort Sumter.* Washington, DC: National Park Service, 1952.
Barrett, John G. *Sherman's March through the Carolinas.* Chapel Hill: University of North Carolina Press, 1956.
Baxley, Neil. *No Prouder Fate: The Story of the 11th South Carolina Volunteer Infantry.* Bloomington, IN: AuthorHouse, 2005.
Bradley, Mark L. *Last Stand in the Carolinas: The Battle of Bentonville.* Campbell, CA: Savas Publishing, 1995.
Capers, Brigadier General Ellison. *Confederate Military History: A Library of Confederate Military History.* 12 Volumes. *Vol. 5. South Carolina.* Edited by Clement Anselm Evans. Atlanta, GA: Confederate Publishing Company, 1899.
Chesnut, Mary Boykin. *A Diary from Dixie.* Edited by Ben Ames Williams. Boston: Houghton Mifflin, 1949.
Coker, Michael D. *The Battle of Port Royal.* Charleston, SC: The History Press, 2009.
Edgar, Walter. *South Carolina: A History.* Columbia: University of South Carolina Press, 1998.

Ellington, Paul *Confederate Flags in the Georgia State Capitol Collection.* Edited by Paul Ellington. Atlanta: Georgia Office of Secretary of State, 1994.

Forman, Robert J. *Bermuda Hundred Campaign Tour Guide.* Chesterfield, VA: Chesterfield Historical Society, 2009.

Hudson, Joshua Hilary. *Sketches and Reminiscences.* Columbia, SC: The State Company, 1903.

Hutson, H.F., and Wm. Henry Trescot. *In Memorium: Gen. Stephen Elliott, Extract from Journal of House of Representatives September 8, 1866.* Columbia, SC: Julian A. Selby, State and City Printer, 1866.

Johnson, John. *The Defense of Charleston Harbor Including Fort Sumter and the Adjacent Islands 1863–1865.* Charleston, SC: Walker, Evans & Cogswell, 1890.

Krick, Robert E.L. *Staff Officers in Gray.* Chapel Hill and London, UK: University of North Carolina Press, 2003.

Ravenel, Samuel W. "The Boy Brigade of South Carolina." *Confederate Veteran* 19 (1901). Nashville, Tennessee.

Roman, Alfred. *The Military Operations of General Beauregard in the War Between the States 1861 to 1865.* New York: Harper and Brothers, 1883.

Schmutz, John F. *The Battle of the Crater: A Complete History.* Jefferson, NC and London, UK: McFarland & Company, 2009.

Trescot, William Henry. *The Late General Stephen Elliott.* London, UK: Sanders, Otley and Company, 1867.

Trudeau, Noah Andre. *The Last Citadel: Petersburg, Virginia June 1864–April 1865.* Baton Rouge: Louisiana State University Press, 1991.

Underwood, Robert Johnson, and Clarence Clough Buel. *Battles and Leaders of the Civil War,* 4 Volumes. New York: The Century Company, 1887–1888.

Wilcox, Arthur M. and Warren Ripley. *The Civil War at Charleston, A Post-Courier Booklet.* Charleston, SC: *The News and Courier* and *The Evening Post,* Eighth edition, 1975.

Wise, Stephen R. *Gate of Hell: Campaign for Charleston Harbor, 1863.* Columbia, SC: 1994.

Witt, W.H., and H.D. Capers. "Flag of the Twelfth Georgia Artillery." *Confederate Veteran* 16 (1908). Nashville, Tennessee.

## Archival Depositories

*Compiled Service Records of Confederate General and Staff Officers, and Nonregimental Enlisted Men, M331* Roll 0085.

# BIBLIOGRAPHY

*Compiled Service Records of Confederate Soldiers Who Served in Organizations From the State of South Carolina, M26,* Rolls 0105, 0155 and 0248. *Confederate Amnesty Papers, Case Files of Applications from Former Confederates for Presidential Pardons ("Amnesty Papers") 1865–1867, M1003,* Roll 0045.
*1860 U.S. Federal Census, Population Schedule, M653,* Roll 1214.
Elliott Family Papers, South Caroliniana Library, University of South Carolina, Columbia, SC.
John Johnson Papers, South Carolina Historical Society, Charleston, SC.
Library of Congress, Prints and Photographs Division, Digital Collections, Washington, DC. https://www.loc.gov.
National Archives:
*Official Records of the Union and Confederate Navies,* 30 Volumes. Washington, DC: U.S. Government Printing Office, 1894–1922.
*The War of the Rebellion: A Compilation of the Official Records of Union and Confederate Armies,* 128 Volumes. Washington, DC; U.S. Government Printing Office, 1880–1891.

## Newspapers

(Anderson, SC) *Intelligencer* \*
(Charleston, SC) *Daily News* \*
(Charleston, SC) *Mercury* \*
(Charleston, SC) *Post and Courier*
(Columbia, SC) *Daily Phoenix* \*
(Columbia, SC) *The State* \*
(Edgefield, SC) *Observer* \*
(Greenville, SC) *Southern Enterprise* \*
(Lancaster, SC) *News* \*
(Philadelphia, PA) *Evening Telegraph* \*
(Richmond, VA) *Daily Dispatch*
(Yorkville, SC) *Enquirer* \*

*Special Note*: Many of these newspapers can be found on microfilm in their respective county libraries or other educational institutions. All are available online. Those marked with * can be found at www.newspapers.com. The Richmond *Daily Dispatch* is available at www.dlxs.richmond.edu, and the Charleston *Post and Courier* is at www.postandcourier.com.

# INDEX

**A**

Averasboro 107

**B**

Barnwell, Stephen Elliott 117, 136
Bay Point 18, 19, 20, 22, 37
Beauregard, General P.G.T. 12, 18, 19, 20, 21, 22, 33, 36, 44, 46, 49, 50, 51, 52, 53, 54, 55, 56, 57, 58, 60, 61, 62, 63, 64, 65, 68, 69, 72, 73, 75, 76, 77, 78, 79, 81, 82, 83, 84, 86, 88, 89, 90, 91, 92, 93, 94, 95, 96, 97, 104, 105, 106, 107, 115, 118, 121, 122, 130, 138
Bentonville, NC 108, 109, 117, 135, 137
Bermuda Hundred Campaign 92, 118, 138
Butler, Benjamin 92

**C**

Champneys, John T. 55, 59, 75
Charleston Battalion 53, 54, 58, 62
Chestnut, Mary Boykin 77, 101, 111, 132, 137
Colcock, Charles J. 31, 32, 103

**D**

Davis, Jefferson 72
Drayton, Thomas 23
Dunovant, Colonel R.G.M. 20, 22, 23

**E**

Elliott, Charlotte 16, 25, 32, 91, 93, 116
Elliott, Henry D. 18, 42, 117
Elliott, John H. 17, 117
Elliott, Middleton Stuart 30, 117
Elliott, Ralph 17, 18, 27, 30, 33, 37, 92, 93, 94, 117

# INDEX

Elliott, Sr., Reverend Stephen 15, 37, 79, 116
Elliott, Stephen Habersham 32
Elliott, William 18, 27, 30, 33, 41, 42, 116

## F

Fort Beauregard 19, 20, 22

## G

Gillmore, Quincy 42, 43, 44, 45, 46, 47, 55, 57, 59, 68, 78, 90, 111, 112, 113
Gilmer, J.F. 49, 63, 79, 121, 122

## H

Howlett Line 94, 96

## J

Johnson, Andrew 111
Johnson, Bushrod 94, 96, 97, 100
Johnson, John 49, 75, 118, 130, 139
Johnston, Joseph 29, 103, 107, 108, 109, 110, 123, 124

## L

Lee, Robert E. 12, 23, 24, 26, 29, 30, 33, 39, 41, 89, 96, 97, 102, 104, 110, 115, 118

## M

McMaster, F.W. 100

Mickler, John H. 31, 32, 129

## P

Pelot, Thomas 18
Pinckney Island 24, 31, 38, 104, 128
Pocotaligo 23, 26, 27, 33, 34, 35, 37, 38, 77, 90, 103, 129

## R

Ravenel, Sam 108, 109, 135, 138
Rhett, Alfred 49

## S

Seddon, J.A. 57, 121
Sherman, W.T. 103, 104, 105, 106, 107, 108, 109, 110, 137
Stuart, Henry M. 30, 39, 104

## T

Taliaferro, W.B. 74, 106, 107, 108
Twelfth Georgia Battalion 65, 68

## U

USS *George Washington* 39, 40, 41, 87

## W

Walker, William S. 12, 26, 90, 118

# ABOUT THE AUTHOR

D. MICHAEL THOMAS is a lifelong student of the War Between the States. He holds a BA in history from The Citadel and is a U.S. Navy veteran of Vietnam. He spent several years as a volunteer of the Chesterfield Historical Society of Virginia, providing research, writing newsletter articles and serving on the board of directors. His first book was *Wade Hampton's Iron Scouts: Confederate Special Forces* (The History Press, 2018).

*Visit us at*
www.historypress.com

www.ingramcontent.com/pod-product-compliance
Lightning Source LLC
Chambersburg PA
CBHW040253170426
43191CB00019B/2397